Guy Hocquenghem

Guy Hocquenghem

Beyond Gay Identity

Bill Marshall

DUKE UNIVERSITY PRESS
DURHAM 1997

First published in the United States in 1997 by
DUKE UNIVERSITY PRESS
Durham, NC 27708–0660
and in the United Kingdom in 1996 by
Pluto Press
345 Archway Road, London N6 5AA

Library of Congress Cataloging-in-Publication Data
Marshall, Bill.
    Guy Hocquenghem / Bill Marshall.
        p.   cm.
    Includes bibliographical references and index.
    ISBN 0–8223–1930–6 (cloth : alk. paper). — ISBN 0–8223–1923–3
(pbk. : alk. paper)
        1. Hocquenghem, Guy, 1946–88.   2. Gay men—France—Biography.
3. Homosexuality—Philosophy.   4. Homosexuality—Political aspects.
I. Title.
HQ75.8.H63M373   1997
305.38'9664—dc20   96–34201
                                                                              CIP

Designed and produced for Pluto Press by
Chase Production Services, Chadlington, OX7 3LN
Typeset from disk by Stanford DTP Services, Milton Keynes
Printed in the E.C. by J. W. Arrowsmith Ltd, Bristol, England

Contents

For Richard

Preface

This is the first monograph on Guy Hocquenghem in English, and seeks to build on previous valuable but brief work on his output by Jeffrey Weeks and Jonathan Dollimore. His name, French but of Flemish origin, is pronounced [ɔkã:gɛm]. It is only in the 1990s that he is gaining a wider audience in the English-speaking world, a process encouraged by the republication in 1993 by Duke University Press of *Homosexual Desire*, and by the proliferation in the United States and to a much smaller extent in Britain of courses and debates in lesbian and gay studies, queer theory, and sexual dissidence. Passing roughly chronologically through his prolific *oeuvre*, which covers a twenty-year period between 1968 and 1988 when he died of an AIDS-related illness, this study seeks to explicate the main lines of his theories and to place them in their French context, while pointing out the way they offer stimulating challenges to orthodox opinion. It is hoped that this brief monograph will contribute to the enhanced presence of Hocquenghem in our debates,[1] not least further translations.

All translations from the French in this text are my own unless otherwise stated. Books in English are published in London, in French in Paris, unless otherwise stated. All works originally published in French are referred to in the text by their French titles; the quotations from them are taken from English editions where these exist.

I would like to thank all those who offered advice, support and suggestions during the writing of this book, especially friends of Guy Hocquenghem such as Olivier Leclair and Lionel Soukaz, but also Richard Dyer, Paul Hamilton, Béatrice Houplain, Annie Janowitz, Jeremy Lane, Sylvie Lindeperg, Keith Reader, Richard Sacker, the superego that was Peter Ucko, and David Vilaseca. Any mistakes are entirely my own. Thanks especially to the School of Research and Graduate Studies in the Faculty of Arts at Southampton University for helping me with teaching relief.

List of Abbreviations

CRA	*Collectif réseau alternatif*
CUARH	*Comité d'urgence anti-repression homosexuel*
FHAR	*Front homosexuel d'action révolutionnaire*
JCR	*Jeunesses Communistes Révolutionnaires*
LCR	*Ligue communiste révolutionnaire*
MLF	*Mouvement de libération des femmes*
MRP	*Mouvement républicain populaire*
PCF	French Communist Party
VLR	*Vive la révolution*

After May

Guy Hocquenghem was born in 1946 into a bourgeois and quasi-intellectual family in Boulogne, just outside the Paris city limits. His mother, who bore ten children, was a French teacher in a girls' *lycée*, his father was a mathematician. Sexually active at the age of 15 with one of his male schoolteachers, Hocquenghem followed an intellectual and political trajectory that then took him through the upper echelons of the French educational system: the prestigious Lycée Henri IV in the Latin Quarter of Paris, and then in 1965 the École Normale Supérieure, France's elite higher education institution devoted to literature and philosophy. A member of the youth wing of the French Communist Party (PCF) from 1962, he left in 1965, joining the Trotskyist JCR (Jeunesses Communistes Révolutionnaires), and publishing articles in its journal, *Avant-garde jeunesse*. He was thus one of the thousands of revolutionary left students who participated in the uprising of May 1968, was active in the occupied Sorbonne, and helped in the production of a short-lived leftist daily newspaper, *Action*.

To understand this early itinerary, what we might call the 'conditions of possibility' of Hocquenghem, and therefore his typicality and atypicality, must be traced sociologically, politically and historically in the context of the quarter century following the end of the Second World War, a period that changed France dramatically and for ever. The combination in the immediate post-war years of Marshall Aid and the governmental planning agency the *Commissariat du Plan* impelled, despite political crises, an average growth rate of 6 per cent of GNP, and a transformation of the economy to one based on generalised mass consumption. For example, between 1954 and 1970 the percentage of French homes with fridges leapt from 7 per cent to 76 per cent, with washing machines from 8 per cent to 53 per cent, with cars 21 per cent to 55 per cent, with television sets from 1 per cent to 66 per cent. As elsewhere in the Western world, this 'modernisation' of French capitalism brought in its wake increased urbanisation, the growth of the mass media, expanded middle and tertiary sectors, eventually an important increase of women in the labour force, the acceleration in the decline of religious belief, and new cultures of individualism. However, in France these changes took place in the context of severe political polarisation. The Second World War had also been a French civil war. The social and economic settlement that followed (social security, national reconstruction) was undermined politically by the lack of consensus around the unstable Fourth Republic (1946–58). Colonial wars raged in Indo-China from 1945 to 1954, in Algeria from 1954 to 1962. While the rivalry between the two political victors of the 1939–45 conflict, Gaullists and Communists, was settled in 1958 by the triumph of the former and the continuation in Cold War ostracism of the latter, Gaullism's success in acting as an ideological transmission-belt between old and new hegemonic formations (decolonisation and economic growth coupled with social conservatism and governmental paternalism) was by the mid-1960s proving to be very fragile. The fruits of prosperity were not evenly distributed. The average working week had actually increased by nearly seven hours between 1938 and 1960, with hourly pay increasing in that time by an average of only 0.6 per cent. De Gaulle himself was forced into a second ballot at the presidential elections of 1965, while the parliamentary left gained considerable ground in elections in 1967.

Hocquenghem's adhesion to the Communists in 1962 (the year of the end of the Algerian war but also for example in February the killing of eight left-wing demonstrators by the police at the Charonne metro station in Paris) can thus be placed in the context of this polarisation as well as, for the left-wing intelligentsia, of the unavoidability of the French Communist Party. Solidly implanted in the working class and far exceeding the electoral strength of a French social democracy tarnished by its colonial record and seemingly in terminal decline, the Party was an obvious but problematic home and resource. While some of the older generation of intellectuals had left with fracas after the suppression of the Hungarian revolution of 1956, the Party continued to recruit well amongst students in the early 1960s. It was not long, however, before its lack of internal democracy and seeming inability to produce an alternative political vision to Stalinism proved too frustrating, and by the mid-decade its support among students had haemorrhaged and its dominance of the students' union ended.[1] The JCR that Hocquenghem joined was one of a myriad of other groups associated with the far left – what the French refer to as *le gauchisme* – that blossomed in the late 1960s. While some were characterised by libertarianism, such as the anarchists, situationists, or Daniel Cohn-Bendit's *Mouvement du 22 mars*, others continued the culture of professional revolutionary militantism in the Marxist tradition, inspired by Trotsky in the case of the JCR, or by Third World revolutionary leaders such as Ho Chi Minh, Che Guevara and especially Mao Zedong.

However, a less well-known post-war history needs to be invoked if we are to understand the discourses available to Hocquenghem in his young adulthood up to May 1968. The French republican tradition born out of 1789 abolished all repressive legislation regarding same-sex activity, and the first explicitly discriminatory legislation dates from the collaborationist Vichy regime in 1942, which established a heterosexual age of consent at 15 and a homosexual at 21, with the penalty of six months to three years imprisonment for its infringement. This law was taken up at the Liberation by De Gaulle's provisional government as paragraph 3 of article 331 of the penal code, just one example of the surprising continuities between Vichy and the post-war period in the matter of the ideological and cultural reconstruction of France.[2] In 1960, the definition of homosexuality as a *fléau social* (social scourge) by the deputy Paul Mirguet led to aggravated punishment for homosexual acts ('act against nature with an individual of the same sex') in cases brought under article 330, namely that of 'outrage public à la pudeur' (the equivalent of 'acts of gross indecency'). So in fact the legal climate for homosexuals in the 1960s became more oppressive.

As Jacques Girard has pointed out,[3] the influence of Catholic opinion weighed heavily in that climate. The Vichy regime had enjoyed widespread support in the Catholic Church, and those Catholics who had fought on the side of the Resistance participated as the MRP (*Mouvement républicain populaire*) in the Liberation governments as well as in the shaky coalitions of the Fourth Republic. In 1960, the fledgling Gaullist Fifth Republic was courting Catholic opinion, and the same year saw an agreement on cooperation between the state and private Catholic school systems. However, it should be added that the left in France, dominated by the Communist Party, was no more receptive to any kind of dissident sexual politics. In this, the Party was firmly in the tradition of Stalinism, for the regime in the USSR in 1934 had introduced draconian anti-homosexual legislation, the first since the overthrow of the Tsarist regime in 1917, as part of a natalist and nationalist outlook.

So although there had been an important gay subculture particularly in Paris in the interwar years, as well as high visibility in artistic circles through the figures of Jean Cocteau, André Gide and later Jean Genet,[4] 1945 was in fact a year zero for homosexual political and cultural identity in France. In 1949, for example, a decree from the head of the Paris police banned dancing between men in public places. The post-war years did however produce homosexual organisations. *Futur* was a newsletter published between 1952 and 1955 which sought to defend homosexuality in the 'scientific' and naturalist tradition of Magnus Hirschfeld and of

Gide's *Corydon* (1924), and thus to take advantage of the massive impact of the Kinsey report. It succumbed to legal harassment on the part of the authorities. *Arcadie* was a magazine launched in 1954 which became the national organisation for homosexuals (or 'homophiles'), with 10 000 subscribers in 1960, and a peak of 40 000 in 1980 (it folded in 1982). Run by a philosophy teacher and former seminarist André Baudry, it eschewed the anticlericalism of *Futur* to embrace a conservative and religious outlook which sought to reconcile French elites with the acceptability of same-sex love. In the late 1960s there would be clashes in its ranks between the conservative old guard and the more liberal and radicalised younger generation, as we shall see.

This is not the moment to enter into a detailed analysis and interpretation of the events of May 1968. Starting in the universities and centring on questions of chronic overcrowding but also the paternalism and authoritarianism of the institution and beyond it the Ministry of Education and the Gaullist state, with opposition to the Vietnam war acting as catalyst in the radicalised world of student politics, the events developed into the biggest and longest general strike in European history, and nearly toppled the regime before De Gaulle retrieved the situation by depicting a red menace and calling parliamentary elections which he easily won. The crisis escapes easy totalisation. At the time, the events were seen as a new type of class struggle involving professionals and experts against bureaucrats and functionaries (Alain Touraine);[5] a carnival or fête during which hierarchies are temporarily overturned only to return in a different form, typical of French history (Raymond Aron);[6] an opportunity for revolution betrayed by the Communist Party, desperate not to be overtaken on its left and to prevent contact between students and workers (for example the syndicalist André Barjonet); and a leftist adventure which would have led to the defeat of the working class and which disrupted the strategy for political change developed by the parliamentary opposition (Waldeck Rochet, leader of the PCF). At the time, Hocquenghem was four-square behind the movement, writing in *Action* that the students' struggle was to 'refuse a University whose sole aim is to forge the bosses of tomorrow and the docile instruments of the economy', and to oppose 'an authoritarian and hierarchical social system'.[7] Sexual matters had been at the forefront of the students' concerns. One of the focuses of protest earlier that year, for example, had been the complete sexual segregation of the halls of residence at Nanterre University. Traditional (Catholic) values were clashing across the generation gap with the demands of young people for sexual autonomy (contraception had been legalised only the previous year, abortion was still completely illegal). In the occupied Sorbonne, carnivalesque venue of free debate, a newly formed homosexual group, the *Comité d'Action Pédérastique Révolutionnaire*, had its posters torn down by *gauchistes*, its attempt to hold meetings frowned upon. Hocquenghem, aware of his double identity as revolutionary militant and active homosexual, later argued that this disappointment, what we might call the last gasp of heterosexism by the French non-Communist left, meant that any impetus for a new homosexual political movement lost three years: 'at the moment when we thought we were at the height of all possible liberation, there were still some aspects of our lives which we weren't allowed to show'.[8]

The years 1968–71 saw Hocquenghem excluded from the JCR in September 1968 along with others in a tendency called 'maos-spontex'. Living communally in the Parisian suburb of Asnières with sexual politics firmly on the agenda, he militated in a group called *Vive la révolution* (VLR), a Maoist[9] group influenced by American counter-culture and interested in questions of lifestyle (hence one meaning of its title). They were to be distinguished from the more purist Maoist militants of the *Gauche prolétarienne*. In 1986 Hocquenghem was to write that he joined 'on the guarantee it was more about anarchism than Maoism',[10] an unsurprising disclaimer given the current consensus about Mao's rule, but also given the reputation of Maoism, like Stalinism, for sexual conservatism. In France as a whole, these years immediately following May 1968 were characterised by continued but isolated confrontations between *gauchistes* and the state, and by a Pompidou presidency attempting timid reforms (the prime minister Jacques Chaban-Delmas's 'new society') but forging ahead with rapid growth and its attendant financial speculations and scandals, all in a still conservative moral climate. For example, Pompidou made a speech in December 1970 in which, not for the first or last time in conservative discourse, 'family values' were invoked as a bulwark founded in nature against the wrenching aspects of 'modernisation' he himself had fostered. (Hocquenghem savaged this in the VLR journal *Tout*,[11] in terms crucial to the sexual-political evolution we are about to examine.) On the mainstream left, the absence of the Communist Party from the May movement, and the *remue-ménage idéologique* the events set in motion, that is the 'ideological moving around or agitation' or new agenda-setting, were to have profound repercussions for the following two decades.

It is at this point, before we see the emergence of a recognisably 'modern' gay movement in France and Hocquenghem's central involvement in its foundation, that it seems useful to compare the post-war histories of France and the USA. There are many similarities: the importance of the Kinsey report in influencing wider public opinion; the groundbreaking role of at first very marginalised but nonetheless overtly pro-homosexual groups, such as the

Mattachine Society and the Daughters of Bilitis in the US; the coexistence in the 1950s of an officially conservative moral climate (Catholicism in France, Eisenhower/McCarthy in the US) with developing consumerism and the undermining of tradition; the dialogue in the late 1960s with feminism and with the (new) new (that is post-Stalinist and initially non-social democratic) left. However, there are crucial differences. In the USA, the Second World War, with its uprooting and combination of homosexual individuals, played a formative role in the construction of the post-war gay identity, and led directly to the settlement of self-consciously gay people in certain cities such as New York and San Francisco, giving rise in turn to a widespread bar subculture. John D'Emilio argues that, unlike cruising in public places with its attendant dangers, in the 1940s 'The bars were seedbeds for a collective consciousness that might one day flower politically.'[12] In France, the Second World War certainly uprooted people, but by and large did not combine them, since the situation was one of Nazi Occupation or collaboration, with vicious laws that specifically targeted homosexuals among others, many of whom were of course deported to death camps. We have seen that the post-war climate was not conducive to bars, and homosexuals would meet, if they did at all, in expensive Parisian clubs, in public cruising spaces at night, or among the placid groves of *Arcadie*.

In addition, the political culture in France was not and is not consistent with the emergence of 'collective consciousness' or group identity as a key player. The Stonewall riots of June 1969 can be seen as part of a very American culture and history that combine traditions of relatively weak national parties, ethnic voting blocks and interest groups, with those of liberal individualism and self-invention. Moreover, as well as the important role played by the American Civil Liberties Union in censorship and other disputes involving homosexuals in the 1950s and 1960s, there was of course the model of the black civil rights movement of the 1960s, a radicalising experience in itself for many later gay activists but one consistent with the demand that full citizenship rights be extended to another self-identified sub-group in the American mosaic. (In fact, the splits in the American gay movement in the early 1970s were largely about race and what attitude to take towards the Black Panthers.) In France, the traditions have been those of republican citizenship, with the key relationship that of the individual and the state with no more than a weak civil society mediating the two if at all, and those of the socialist left, which have sought either to extend the gains of the Revolution to the industrial working class (roughly, the socialist or social-democratic heritage since Jean Jaurès), or to surpass the Republic in the dialectical movement of a revolution (the Communists and the *gauchistes*, supposedly).

Needless to say, a 'modern' gay movement in, respectively, 1969 and 1971, emerges in the two countries on to radically different terrains, whatever subsequent developments might hold. Initially but crucially, Hocquenghem's principal interlocutors via the FHAR (*Front homosexuel d'action révolutionnaire*) are the *gauchistes*. In 1977, Hocquenghem argued that the specificities of the French context and the resulting tardiness of homosexual politics there (due to the intellectualisation of dissident debates, the isolation of Paris, the culture of 'proletarian terrorism' prevalent in the *gauchiste* camp), were in fact advantageous, in that homosexual politics addressed first the counter-society of militants rather than official society, which meant from the start that the revolutionary potential of that politics was stressed, rather than demands for integration.[13]

The new sexual politics of the early 1970s was both enabled by the May 1968 movement (particularly its *remue-ménage idéologique*) and a reaction against its machismo and heterosexism. These contradictions rhymed with the transformations of the 1960s in general, which saw the beginnings of the delegitimation of traditional gender roles, but also the intensification of the sexual objectification of women. Where the *Mouvement de libération des femmes* (MLF) in 1970 prolonged May's emphasis on anti-authority and direct action while developing a distinct political discourse placing gender oppression at the centre, the new homosexual movement followed. Some of the female members of *Arcadie* (350 women to 11 500 male members at that time) had developed links with the MLF, and, strongly influenced by the development of the Gay Liberation Front in the USA, were joined in their discussion group by male homosexuals, including Hocquenghem. Joint direct action was organised against an anti-abortion meeting in Paris on 5 March 1971, and five days later against a broadcast debate on 'homosexuality, that distressing problem'. In the process, the FHAR was born, organising weekly meetings at the Paris Fine Arts School, distributing tracts in gay meeting-places. Their reflections were published in the historic twelfth issue of *Tout* in April, which rapidly became the best-selling issue of any *gauchiste* journal of the time. Unsold issues were eventually seized by the authorities and legal action taken against its director, Jean-Paul Sartre, at that time a fellow-travelling Maoist.

The basic texts of the FHAR are collected in its *Rapport contre la normalité*, published in 1971, and in a collection of Hocquenghem's essays entitled *L'Après-mai des faunes*/The After-May of the Fawns, published in 1974. The account that follows seeks to parallel the triple structure of the latter, which frames the original texts with Hocquenghem's comments on his former positions.

First, the chronology of the collection suggests a teleology, and invites a reading between the lines of Hocquenghem's writings between 1968 and 1971 so as to discern the emerging discourse of homosexual politics through the Maoist orthodoxies. Thus an article in *Révolution culturelle* in June 1969 argues against the separation of work, private life and leisure, and (taking China as the model ...) for getting beyond the mere seizure of the bourgeois state apparatus which, as in Eastern Europe, 'makes the counter-revolution's bed'.[14] In April 1970, Hocquenghem, still invoking Mao, entitles an article 'Changer la vie' ('Change life', a discourse of personal *revolt* in contrast with the 'transform the world' of orthodox Marxism), in which he lambasts the family as the 'pillar of oppression' and argues against the militant self-repression which falsely models itself on the 'disciplined proletarian', and danger-ously presents the masses with a model of the family as sole possible and imaginable way of living:

> The two paths before us today are clear: change the individual by inoculating him with the proletarian vaccine that will immunise him by a fantastic self-repression against his own desires, or else change the situation and relations inside the group and between the group and the masses.[15]

The counter-culture (Joplin, Hendrix, drugs) is defended in the name of creativity (the risk of the bourgeoisie setting the terms of the new culture) and of 'life': 'The revolution is not what allows us to replace life.'[16] Even the revolt of East against West Pakistan becomes part of an argument in favour of proceeding from the particular to the universal rather than the dogmatic reverse (China of course supported the latter in the conflict, hence some acrobatics from orthodox Maoists like André Glucksmann): 'Revolutionary analysis is universal in that its point of departure is the particular, and not when it refuses the particular as *abnormal*.'[17]

The moment of the FHAR, then, was a departure both from existing *gauchiste* politics and from previous homosexual 'politics'. It identified the oppression of homosexuals as systematic, in the strict sense as part of a system of gender domination within capitalism. Boldly, it was thus able to recentre that oppression within the discourse of *gauchisme* itself: 'it [the FHAR] was a political world which resembled an upside-down pyramid, since it was about reversing an order of things in which we were considered to be at the extreme margins'.[18] Several elements combined. The critique of capitalism targeted the couple and the family, their complicity with bourgeois relations of property, hierarchy and labour. The direct personal action of 'coming out' spoke to the counter-cultural priority of revolt and personal liberation, as well as locking into the French post-war existentialist discourse of authenticity: 'We don't choose to be homosexual, we find ourselves with a label stuck on our backs with people laughing at some of our intonations. We don't choose to be homosexual, but we choose to remain so.'[19] At the same time, there were echoes of the French revolutionary and republican tradition: those *gauchistes* who refused to address sexual questions were like those revolutionaries in the 1890s who insisted the Dreyfus case was a bourgeois matter.[20] Indeed, the movement from the particular to the universal noted earlier, while it is a riposte to the *gauchistes*, seems also to be a reinscription of the French revolutionary idea of the 'particular' French nation bearing a universal message to the world: 'it's precisely because he [the 'conscious homosexual'] lives and thus accepts the most *particular* situation that what he thinks has a *universal* value'.[21]

It is however the relationship between men and women which proved to be the most fragile element of the discursive coalition that formed the FHAR. While the MLF's dialogue with the FHAR lasted considerably longer than with the *gauchistes*, it was limited by the historical context, lack of conceptual development, and the very instability of the interpellations and identities evoked by the term 'homosexual'. Contradictions debated in the initial euphoria (the idea that male homosexuals in patriarchy betray male society while lesbians are oppressed as women), or the agreement around the term *phallocratisme* which for Hocquenghem can be used to settle accounts with the Maoists,[22] soon dissipate in disputes around sex and love. While the women's experience of the 1960s led them to a perception of sex with men as contaminated with the oppressions of patriarchy, for homosexual men one of the main aims of their movement was to desublimate sex in an uninhibited and thus 'liberated' fashion (as the FHAR meetings became until they were closed by police in 1972). Hocquenghem in the space of just over a year articulates the positive aspects of love between homosexuals and lesbians ('Only the bourgeois can imagine that true love is realised in a prick thrusting into a vagina')[23], while later distancing himself from such an idea in the name of men as 'orgasm machines'.[24]

The shortcomings of the FHAR need not blind us to its achievements, the most lasting of which was to force reflection about homosexual politics and thus to place it firmly on the agenda, not only of *le gauchisme*, but of the renascent Socialist Party and even the Communists. What a contrast there is between the veteran Communist leader Jacques Duclos's riposte to a FHAR militant in 1972 ('You third sex people are all sick and abnormal'),[25] and the begrudging but evolved position of the Party in 1977.[26]

Hocquenghem's own personal 'discursive coalition' does not take long to unravel or to 'drift', to employ the metaphor of his 1977 collection of essays, *La Dérive homosexuelle/The Homosexual Drift*. The third procedure of the *L'Après-mai des faunes* had indeed been that of the undermining and surpassing of his previous positions via the italicised text written in 1974. The structure of that collection is at one with Hocquenghem's epistemology (in the sense of the philosophical grounding of his knowledge), to be discussed in the chapter that follows this. However, even in the 1971 texts it was clear that a politics of fixed or even stable identity was not the aim. This could be expressed somewhat inchoately, as when he accepts the label or performance of effeminacy as a revolt against the 'norms' of machismo: 'We lay claim to our 'femininity' even as women reject theirs, at the same time as we declare these roles to have no meaning.'[27] At the same time, the emphasis of the FHAR on the ultimate aim of abolishing social and sexual norms could be harnessed to an effective call for the radicality of instability: 'Our incoherence, our instability frighten the bourgeois ... At any moment, we can bring a critical eye to bear on ourselves, because we don't know any more what "ourselves" in fact means.'[28]

In the 1974 texts which frame the earlier essays in *L'Après-mai des faunes*, Hocquenghem critiques his and the FHAR's former reliance on a discourse of humanism and the unified self, the 'gay [*pédés*] jacobins' promoting a '1789 of sex': 'it's still a body of the self, less liberated than devoted to liberalism, which the new slogans reveal', the 'humanism of a sexual *habeas corpus* which leaves to one side the richest aspects of social sexualisation'. The unproblematised unified self of liberalism, when harnessed to a group identity, a 'we', slides into what is by 1974 the ultimate horror: 'that prop, that corset of the homosexual thirsting for dignity, at the height of its totalitarian delirium'.[29] So even by 1973–74, Hocquenghem is not where he might be expected to be. Having participated in the establishment of a homosexual voice in French politics, he spends much of his time undermining the certainties – 'the bright agora of sexual identity'[30] – on which that voice might be based. So not for him, for example, the integration of homosexuals in the military (because the whole system is based on the sublimation of same-sex desire),[31] nor, invoking Proust, the desire to rebuild Sodom in a prioritising of 'homosexual' self-assertion:[32] 'Our homosexuality is not a revolutionary value to be extended to the whole world, but a permanent questioning.'[33]

Hocquenghem's dissatisfaction with the developing 'gay movement' in the 1970s, even as it succeeded in entering the public sphere (for example on the film and discussion programme *Les Dossiers de l'écran*, watched by 19 million viewers in January 1975, with guests including the novelists Jean-Louis Bory and Yves Navarre, as well as André Baudry and Paul Mirguet) with Hocquenghem himself taking on that public role of 'representative' or 'embodied concept',[34] is elucidated in the collection of essays *La Dérive homosexuelle*, published in 1977. His contention is that the commercialisation of homosexuality has simply led to a reorganisation of the private and of relations of power in society. The

'homosexual revolution' is in this sense no more a revolution than
that of the motor car, in that while it is altering interpersonal
relations it is simply the tip of a new social-sexual model, defining
new margins and centres, which is freezing the positions won since
1971. There are two targets here. First, 'homosexual identity' is
becoming limited to, and is indeed a sub-category within, consumerism: 'The time will come when the homosexual will be no
more than a sex tourist, a nice Club-Med member who has been
a bit further than the rest, whose horizon of pleasure is a bit broader
than his average contemporary.'[35] Hocquenghem seeks to escape
this configuration that segregates on the grounds of class, race, age
and power, 'this movement of closure which is founding new
sexual bourgeoisies':[36]

> As I drifted in one direction, trying to connect with the ocean
> of the unformulated, exploring the scarcely specific margins of
> homosexualities, Homosexuality, now acknowledged, was
> moving in the other: organising, rationalising, not only appro-
> priated but moreover founding new values and why not new
> empires. Becoming the herald of new repressions, demanding
> the punishment of gay-bashing hooligans and the integration
> of homosexuals into the American army and police. Becoming
> substance, acquiring a body and a culture.[37]

More surprisingly, the other target, complicit with this reconfigu-
ration of middle-class consumer culture, is the women's movement,
particularly, but not only, radical feminism. Even in 1973,
Hocquenghem had seen the MLF, in its critique of male sexuality,
as an agent of moral rearmament, a vehicle for totalising and
simplistic gender statutes (including men's guilt for being men) which
continued the discursive structures of Maoism, with the signifier
'women' replacing that of 'proletariat'.[38] Just as gay men have
begun to appeal to the 'good' repression of the state, the anti-sex
attitudes of some feminists have led them, mistakenly for
Hocquenghem, to follow a similar path of complicity with dominant
power. This line of argument culminates in a, to say the least,
provocative article ('V-I-O-L'/'R-A-P-E') in *Libération* in March
1977,[39] which castigates the feminists for campaigning against an
impecunious Arab student accused of rape. While sharing the
indignation and acknowledging that the victim suffered terrible
violence, Hocquenghem first asks why the penetrating penis
represents a qualitatively different violence from acts of stabbing
or burning, and argues that the vocabulary of the 'sacred' circu-
lating around this incident of 'defloration' is an abstract and
intangible principle which is being invoked to justify state repression.
    Several questions arise here, needless to say, but it must be said
that the sentences that follow bear out Hocquenghem's tactic of

provocation. As any feminist would argue, Hocquenghem is neglecting the whole symbolic order of sexual difference which means that the penis represents power, patriarchy, male domination. Rape is the *summum* of this system. Hocquenghem, anticipating this, asks why the anus does not possess the same symbolic (or 'transcendent') power as the vagina (a point more fully developed in his theoretical work *Le Désir homosexuel*), but undermines the point by burying it in a sentence about (gay) men not making a similar fuss about being raped (which begs other questions, symbolic, cultural and legal). His wish to get beyond binary thought and the humanism of the feminists, and his assertion of the polymorphousness of desire, nonetheless still seem to prevent him from embracing a true problematisation of gender. Writing elsewhere in 1977, a sentence like 'gay men [*les pédés*] are sexual obsessives'[40] is not only highly totalising, rejoining the 'we' he had earlier critiqued, but logically implies that no homosexual man can occupy the feminist position of not prioritising physical desire. What phrase more redolent of binary gender thought is that which he uses in the article on rape to describe the feminists: 'their chorus of hysterical denouncers'? Despite these obvious but telling shortcomings, that article does at least succeed in asking questions about not simply the coincidence of some feminist and conservative discourse but moreover the coexistence (around different crimes) in much liberal or progressive thought of notions of both retribution and seeking to understand the causes of criminality.

If recourse to the state is not the way forward, if he is opposing homosexual positivity, and if his pluralism has its gender limitations, then what is Hocquenghem's project? The answer is that it is becoming primarily an ethical and aesthetic one which cultivates the margins of homosexuali*ties*, those non-totalisable practices which fall through the system, such as *les folles* (camp or drag queens), 'on the frontier between art and life, outside politics',[41] 'that patchwork of street culture, art, preciosity and vulgarity which formed the complex tissue of a mode of apprehending the world without dullness or common sense',[42] and delinquency. However, he also seeks to challenge the homo-hetero binary, as well as the segregation of generations to be found in the discursive system surrounding children's sexuality: 'When you look at the desiring relations between majors and minors, you touch the system of distribution that cuts the child from the adult in all of us, and which segregates them in the social body.'[43] (It should be noted that the FHAR's opposition to the age of consent was based on questions of equality and a critique of the family, and that Hocquenghem's phrase has much wider implications.)[44]

While these themes are developed in later chapters of this study, it is worth invoking another provocative article from *Libération* in the late 1970s, this time on the murder of Pasolini in November 1975, in order to begin to explore the importance for him of that other marginality, delinquency and criminality. In 'Tout le monde ne peut pas mourir dans son lit'/'Not everyone can die in their beds',[45] Hocquenghem's main point is not to join in the chorus of indignation against Pasolini's murderer, but to ask the question why Pasolini himself chose to run the risk of a violent death in his search for sexual encounters. Again, the argument is against an integrative view of homosexuality, which, 'reducing it to love between the Same, shuts itself into a closed and hierarchical tautology', and in favour of 'a flight towards the Others, towards others, even at the risk of dying'. Thus the categorisation of homosexuality as delinquency and criminality is preferable, for example, to that of (psychiatric) deviancy, and a lifestyle involving encounters with people unlike oneself is preferable to the contemporary neutralisation of same-sex desire and its attendant conformities. Hocquenghem seeks to avoid the charge that he is complicit here in blaming Pasolini as much as his killer (the fact that for the police and judicial system killer and homosexual victim melt into one seedy milieu is part of his argument), but admits to the nostalgia inherent in his own position.

Aside from the volumes of essays discussed here, Hocquenghem in the late 1970s was gaining media prominence in his role, recalcitrantly played, of public homosexual: a collaboration in 1977 with Bory entitled *Comment nous appelez-vous déjà?: Ces hommes que l'on dit homosexuels*/What Do You Call Us Again?: The Men They Call Homosexuals; a role as *suppléant* – reserve – candidate for a homosexual list in the eighteenth *arrondissement* of Paris at the parliamentary elections of 1978; a film and book produced with Lionel Soukaz in 1979 on the history of homosexuality (*Race d'Ep! Un siècle d'images de l'homosexualité*). He also completed in 1979 a long essay on French nationalism, *La Beauté du métis: réflexions d'un francophobe*/The Beauty of Mixed Blood: Reflections of a Francophobe. His main activity was a journalistic one on the newspaper *Libération*. Set up in 1971 by Sartre, this quintessentially post-1968 organism was evolving into the mainstream of French political and cultural life, and can be seen as a paradigm of the hegemonic shifts occurring in French society in the 1970s.

While May 1968 had failed to produce short-term political change, its agendas and also its failure were to have longer-term repercussions in the broadest cultural sense. Feminism, ecology, and a general libertarianism produced discourses which were taken up by differing political traditions in a competition for hegemony in French society. A former prime minister, Pierre Mendès France, declared in an interview in 1978:

You must see today that all political formations are dealing with questions that were previously taboo. Young people, women, immigrants, prisoners, ecology: they are the products of May '68 ... May '68 has deeply imbued all those with responsibility in the country.[46]

Valéry Giscard d'Estaing, the youngish (48) centrist and former finance minister under De Gaulle, was narrowly elected president in 1974 as the candidate of prudent change against the Socialist-Communist alliance led by François Mitterrand. Giscard's project had been to channel social dissent into the construction of a consensual liberalised society in a modernised capitalist economy on the model of West Germany, but it foundered through a combination of the economic crisis, his reliance on Gaullists for a parliamentary majority, and his own vanity. A bill legalising abortion was passed in the National Assembly in November 1974 only because it was supported by the left. As one example of the failure of Giscardian liberalism, posters and advertising for the magazine *Gaie-Presse* were banned in March 1978, leading to its collapse.

It was the renewed Socialist Party under Mitterrand which was the main repository in the 1970s of post-1968 discourses, and, having weakened the Communists but still in alliance with them, it was able to capitalise on Giscard's failure, sway important sections of the new middle sectors, and win the elections of 1981. The discourses of 1968 and after mingled with those of the 1940s' Liberation period to produce a cocktail of nationalisations and social reform. A Ministry of Women's Rights was created, the police were enjoined to cease discrimination against homosexuals, the minister of the interior received a delegation from the CUARH (*Comité d'urgence anti-repression homosexuel*), and on 27 July 1982 the infamous paragraph 2 of article 331 was abolished, with an equal age of consent established for homosexual and heterosexual acts. However, the Socialist government's reflationary attempt at 'Keynesianism in one country' provoked inflation, a balance of payments crisis and a run on the franc, and a return to financial orthodoxy was instituted as early as 1982. In 1984, Pierre Mauroy, the 'old left' prime minister and mayor of the northern industrial city of Lille was replaced by the young technocrat Laurent Fabius, and it is around this point that can be dated one of the most profound post-war hegemonic shifts in French society. A new consensus based on competitivity and economic and technical 'modernisation' meant that the '*patrons*'/'bosses' became '*des chefs d'entreprises*'/'heads of companies'. It seemed that by the end of their first five years, the Socialists had achieved that *décrispation*, that calming of social tensions and depolarisation of political debate around an efficiently and 'fairly' managed capitalism, that had so eluded Giscard.

I have dwelt on these political changes because they are the scene for Hocquenghem's reflections on the fate of homosexual and in general post-1968 politics and culture in this kind of individual-centred consumer society, and especially for his 1986 book lambasting the 1968 generation, *Lettre ouverte à ceux qui sont passés du col Mao au Rotary/Open Letter to Those who Have Gone from the Mao Collar to the Rotary Club*. This was his first booklength inter-vention of the period, the earlier part of the decade having been devoted to his novel-writing. The work is rich not just in very Parisian satire, but also in the way it sets an agenda for his other works on philosophy and history, and moreover in its implications for what meaning we can attribute to the Socialist governments of 1981–86, and their relationship to the hopes of May 1968.

It is at this point that we can usefully invoke the cultural historian Pascal Ory's notion of 'generation', in the sense of an age group (bearing in mind the heterogeneities of class and gender) 'charac-terised by a complex of events that do not so much found but crystallise, in which the event fertilises or enriches the structural'.[47] Thus the central events for those entering maturity in 1945–55 were the Liberation and the Cold War; for 1955–65 the Algerian war and the birth of the Fifth Republic; for 1965–75 May 1968; for 1975–85 the economic crisis and the wane of Communism/Marxism. Flourishing on the twin crises of Gaullism and *gauchisme* in the early 1970s, the *soixante-huitards*, following May, were embodying 'a fragile synthesis between two radicalisms, those of formal and political revolution, which can be translated as a simultaneous aspiration towards a maximum of freedom in a maximum of identity',[48] and in their various specialised leftisms were able to mobilise symbolic operations and representations (demonstrations, cultural texts). The resulting movement of cultural liberation contributed to the end of the specificity of French political polarisation, and became 'a French modality of the great leap into social relativity'.[49] By the late 1970s and early 1980s, many of that generation had become installed in 'spaces of cultural legitimation'.[50] (As an example of one of these spaces, the magazine *Globe*: 'A generation that is inaugurating the encounter between the left and capitalism, technology and dreams, business and creation.')[51]

These, especially the ex-Maoists, are the targets of Hocquenghem's satire, rather than those like Daniel Cohn-Bendit, whose German Green credentials are deemed to be acceptable,[52] or the unnamed Alain Krivine, the Trotskyist from the JCR days (now LCR – *Ligue communiste révolutionnaire*, which in the 1970s was the far left group most amenable to dialogue with the homosexual activists).[53] While the Socialist government is largely abominated in his text, it is those former *gauchistes* and other left-wingers who have rallied to it, rallied in other words to power, who suffer the often *ad*

hominem invective. These are especially Serge July, editor of
Libération, 'the *Pravda* of the new bourgeois';[54] Roland Castro,
former VLR Maoist and now the Elysée's official architect with a
social conscience; Bernard Kouchner, founder of *Médecins sans
frontières*; and the now anti-Marxist 'new philosophers' of the late
1970s who rallied first to Giscard then to Mitterrand: Bernard-Henri
Lévy and Hocquenghem's former Maoist comrade André
Glucksmann. The abstractions Hocquenghem savages include:
power, *le look*, repudiation of former positions (*le reniement*, a
renegade show of free thought which is in fact a ritual of social integration foreclosing others' dissent),[55] money, hypocrisy, careerism,
conformism, *arrivisme*, the state, neo-liberalism, the valorisation of
Father/Authority/the Law, guilt, consensus ('not neither left nor
right, but a concentration of the worst of the two'),[56] opportunism,
the prosaic, the mediocre, kitsch.

   I wish to concentrate on two sets of semes (in the sense of
minimal elements of meaning) and follow them through
Hocquenghem's argument in order to analyse how their elements
interlink, and how suggestive they are of his underlying assumptions and of the possible positive terms of his discourse. The first
is what we might call the masculinity/machismo–war–nationalism–authority nexus. Hocquenghem's ire is directed towards those
intellectuals who supported the government's stance in the early
1980s on the installation of Cruise and Pershing missiles in Western
Europe, the French army's intervention in Chad, and the sinking
of the Greenpeace ship, the *Rainbow Warrior*: the ex-Stalinist Yves
Montand, but also July's *Libération*, with its 'secondary power's
"Falklands complex"'.[57] André Glucksmann's *La Bêtise*/Stupidity
of 1985 pleaded for the atom bomb and the rearming of Europe
in defence of 'civilisation', an argument that for Hocquenghem leads
him, in his condemnation of the German Greens, into a typically
French xenophobia. *Libération*, Marguerite Duras and much of the
French intelligentsia rallied around the defence minister Charles
Hernu over the *Rainbow Warrior* in August–September 1985.[58] It
is in this context that the *ad hominem* aspect of Hocquenghem's
discourse – notably the attack on July's physical appearance – can
be understood, as this warmongering is also represented as an
unresolved crisis of masculinity inherited from the *Gauche prolétarienne* era, 'whose anti-feminism and clandestine homosexualism
of machos together (with them everything was clandestine) led to
their hatred of their own physical selves, and the absence of humour
towards their own bodies'.[59]

   The second set of semes is what we might call the nexus of
realism–utilitarianism–indifference–spectacle–modernisation–post-
modern orthodoxy. If May 1968 was the stuff of youth and dreams,
his targets are

professional ideologues of realism, 'supporters of what exists' (Lyotard's expression); half-erudites, cut-price aesthetes, discoverers of the obvious, you can never fasten yourselves enough to the real, adhere to it, support it. You have turned yourselves into the apostles of the useful.[60]

Their aesthetics are 'at a distance, devoid of both passion and disinterest, basely preoccupied with proclaiming their own sophistication',[61] colluding with the spectacular aspects of contemporary life in which there is no engagement and, by implication, if we recall the classic situationist text of 1967, Guy Debord's *La Société du spectacle*/Society of the Spectacle, an alienating lack of democratic control and empowerment. The orthodoxy of the Fabius administration, that of 'modernisation', has killed off 'the inventive spirit of the modern',[62] and is simply code for 'the organisation of unemployment'.[63] This invocation of the 'modern' is opposed to the orthodoxies surrounding the 'post-modern', and it is these orthodoxies, rather than a sustained analysis of the term, which Hocquenghem criticises: a dispersion and breaking up of ideologies, a faith only in narrow scientific causalities.

If these are the villains, who are the heroes, what are the positive terms? The mix is eclectic: Sartre, Genet, Adorno, Baudrillard, Nietzsche; utopianism, imagination, art, passion. Sartre is the father-figure abandoned and indeed vilified by the *gauchistes* in favour of new ones such as Mitterrand; Hocquenghem, without too much adulation, judges him to have a positive balance-sheet, the 'uselessly generous'[64] intellectual who never rallied to power, and he does not forget his role in defending the FHAR edition of *Tout* in 1971. Genet never repudiated his criminal past despite his literary success. Adorno is used to differentiate a 'modern' associated with dissent and negative dialectics from a contemporary 'modernisation' which views 'the new as an empty stereotype, an assembly-line repetition of fashion'.[65] Nietzsche is used to criticise state-subsidised theatre director Patrice Chéreau's pompous staging of Wagner. And Baudrillard, far from being seen as an apologist for the 'post-modern' real, is used to demonstrate that the collapse of former left ideologies is not an excuse to embrace neo-liberalism and nationalism: 'Demythify, not remythify',[66] the avoidance of myths of European 'identity'.[67] Hocquenghem is therefore coming from a position based on ethics ('More than ideological betrayal, it is a question here of an attitude of the spirit, a disposition of the soul'),[68] and aesthetics. The official and bureaucratic art of culture minister Jack Lang, who 'needed to transform that nebulous ideal of the *Fête* and its spontaneous, egalitarian utopianism into *fêtes* of Power',[69] is thus an art devoid of its 'insolent and corroding power'.[70] Clearly, Hocquenghem is seeking to reconnect with a dissident, Romantic, even dandy notion of art, 'the aristocratic need for utopia'.[71]

The philosophical assumptions behind this will be explored in subsequent chapters. Suffice it to say that we are not going to get a pragmatic politics from this discourse, and that is in a way his point. Sometimes he is acute in his critical analysis, as when he argues that the methods and mental structures of Maoism persist in the new orthodoxy, even to the point of Gilbert Castro declaring that Mao taught him business.[72] For there is a totalitarian anti-totalitarianism in the new orthodoxies:

> The absolute real of our media, characterised by the expansion of communication for communication's sake, *is* an ideology, whereas Soviet Marxism is basically just a hidden pragmatism. The valorisation of individual careers at any price, the aestheticism of the philistine, narrow scientism, philosophical eclecticism, oppressive and superficial altruism, cynicism and a nomenklatura all prosper both in Moscow and St-Germain-des-Prés.[73]

In this way, the evolution of these *soixante-huitards* simply repeats intellectual events of the post-war years, for example those surrounding Arthur Koestler and the *God that Failed* group. (The political but also theoretical challenge is to think beyond these binaries, and we shall see Hocquenghem grappling with this problem.) However, not only does Hocquenghem repeat some binary gender concepts (criticising the warmongerers as 'feminine pessimists, hysterical nihilists'),[74] the dilemma of his very intervention is that it is in itself a media event among Parisian bourgeois intellectuals debating with each other. Nor does he convince when he attempts to argue against the new consensus while himself asserting that even May 1968 was 'neither right nor left'.[75] And he leaves unclear the difference between the repudiations of the 'renegades' and the changes and inconsistencies of his own position, an evolving one as we have seen. 'It is difficult to disavow your homosexuality' once you have come out, he proclaims,[76] but his relationship to his sexuality in 1986 is radically different from that of 1971. He himself wrote in 1973, apropos of homosexuals but consistent with his view of the self, 'We do not aim at being faithful to ourselves, in an eternal self-resemblance.'[77] He rightly berates *Libération* for its coverage of AIDS (as a 'gay cancer', the sensationalising of Rock Hudson 'the AIDS star'),[78] but his critique of its hypocritical hide-and-seek game around the cause of Michel Foucault's death in 1984 raises uncomfortable questions about Hocquenghem's own secrecy about his condition. Such coverage may partly explain his attitude, but it could also be seen as a collusion with the media's agenda. In the end, Hocquenghem's own distancing from the discourses of 1968–71, his perception of the demise of that 'old story, commitment' (in French, the Sartrean *engagement*), and as early as 1974 his emphasis on 'positions' and 'localisations' rather than 'just struggles' and 'the great questions which preoccupy humanity',[79] render all the more urgent the work of developing counter-discourses sufficiently contradictory of the orthodoxies of the Parisian media.

It is thus clear that the implications of May 1968 go much further than the short term of a political crisis or the medium term of governmental change and hegemonic discourses under the Socialists. Some interpreters of the May events have emphasised the ways in which the discourses of Marxism and revolution simply constituted the available vocabulary for cultural renewal within the terms of the capitalist system, and that the barricades invoking 1848 and 1871 were simply a *mise en scène*. May was thus the high-water mark of Marxist and revolutionary discourse in France, ushering in the 1970s' and 1980s' society of individualism, autonomy and hedonism. This is the argument of, for example, the journalist Laurent Joffrin when comparing May 1968 to the demonstrations of December 1986.[80] Régis Debray (who had accompanied Che Guevara for part of the 1960s and who spent three years in a Bolivian prison), in his pamphlet excoriating, on the tenth anniversary in 1978, the official appropriations of the events, goes further and argues that May 1968 was the cradle of the new bourgeois society, in which the France of economic modernisation and the France of traditional hierarchical culture clashed, the culture thus adjusting to the new technological and economic realities. A ruse of history meant that the students in 1968 thus ushered in the renewal of French capitalism:

> Just as Hegelian great men are what they are because of the world spirit, the May revolutionaries were the entrepreneurs of the spirit needed by the bourgeoisie. The fault was not theirs, but that of the universe in which people do not choose to be born: they accomplished the opposite of what they intended.[81]

While it is difficult to overestimate the changes in French society since 1945 and indeed 1968 (Pascal Ory remarks that on a certain number of ethical questions, the period 'marks the most important upheaval in the entire history of the country since Clovis, if not to say Cro-Magnon man'),[82] it is fair to say that the fear Hocquenghem expressed when he was defending the counter-culture in 1971 and emphasising the need for the *soixante-huitards* to participate in the construction of the new, namely that the bourgeoisie would get there first, has largely come to pass.

This poses three challenges to Hocquenghem's thought, three pathways for us to explore. First, there is the question of the capacity of the system to correct itself, given the instability but also flexibility and adaptability of capitalism. Just as Jacques Derrida, in his critique of logocentrism and the metaphysical in the Western philosophical tradition, explores their limits but cannot in language get beyond them, so is Hocquenghem faced with the possibility of even his own former militant activities contributing to that ushering in of 1980s' 'realism'.

Secondly, the aftermath of May 1968 raises questions around historical and cultural periodisation, and the meanings of the terms 'modernity' and 'post-modernity'. For example, the sociologist Gilles Lipovetsky argues that the contemporary post-modern culture of personalisation, individualism, fluidity, destandardisation and hedonism, which represents such a break from the modern paradigms of history, revolution, standardisation and the disciplinary, was there at the beginning in 1968, for the May movement was in fact 'a relaxed and even laxist movement, the first indifferent revolution';[83] a 'revolution without a historical project, May '68 is a cool uprising without deaths, a "revolution" without revolution, a movement of communication as much as a social confrontation'.[84] The new social movements of feminism and homosexual politics contributed to that loosening of categories and identities within the paradigms of consumerism. By the 1980s (and so well before the fall of Communism in 1989–91), the social-democratic tradition was already in crisis, hence the difficulties of the Socialist governments of the 1980s. For Hocquenghem, there are thus urgent questions to ask about the relationship between 'modern' and 'post-modern', and how to think beyond them.

Thirdly and relatedly, it is possible to read the failed society and culture of the 1980s in the Hegelian dialectical terms of master and slave. This is the implication of Régis Debray's analysis, and it haunts Hocquenghem's evaluation of the new homosexual 'identity' as early as 1973: 'as if the whole journey since May could be summarised in the shift from the world of slaves to the world of dissolute masters'.[85] What is thus needed is a different epistemology, and this is already beginning to take shape, if that is the word, in *L'Après-mai des faunes*. Here the key terms are *volutions* and *transversalisme*. *Volution* is opposed to the totalising linearity of 'revolution', and this has profound implications for the category 'homosexual' and for homosexual politics, as Gilles Deleuze points out in his preface: 'a very mobile spiral ... At one level he can say yes, yes I am homosexual, at another level no that isn't it, at another it's something else again.'[86] The solid, existential, homosexual subject of 1971–2 is for Hocquenghem by 1977 no more: 'homosexuality is here just the name for a now dead segment in a line of force in transversal displacement'.[87] This is tricky ground, given the nature of the system, and Hocquenghem's early justification for this project perhaps unconsciously reveals its dangers: 'This transversalisation is a response to [but the French 'répondre à' can also mean 'correspond to'] capital's war of movement, its fluid and instant displacement from one continent to the other through the activities of multinationals, and thus to its ungraspable character.'[88] Given these challenges, we shall now see on what bases are constructed Hocquenghem's theories of desire and sexuality.

2

Desire

Readers immersed in the theoretical debates prevalent in the humanities in the Anglo-Saxon world may be surprised by Hocquenghem's targets in the *Lettre*. For instead of the main intellectual challenges to Marxism to be found on the left, namely 'post-structuralism' or 'post-modernism', we find in France in the 1980s orthodoxies of neo-liberalism associated with Glucksmann and Lévy. In a telling phrase, Hocquenghem refers to these orthodoxies as those of the 'old subject' and 'old machinism',[1] that in fact modern confidence in unified subjectivity and technical progress which he will seek to surpass. It is commonplace to say that the neo-liberalism of the 1980s marks the victory of Raymond Aron over the Marxist Existentialist tradition represented by Sartre. Absent from this narrative are the currents of structuralism and post-structuralism hegemonic on the intellectual left since about the mid-1970s (for example the journal *Tel Quel* shifted its allegiance from China to the USA in 1974). This set of very diverse thinkers, including Baudrillard, Foucault and Lyotard, some of whose theoretical work accommodates to the new social and political realities of the 1980s, nonetheless represent a much more serious challenge both to the Hegelianised Marxism typified by the figure of Sartre and born out of the political urgencies of the 1930s, the Second World War and the Cold War, and to most of the assumptions of the neo-liberal consensus.

In order to locate Hocquenghem's theoretical work of 1972, *Le Désir homosexuel/Homosexual Desire*, within this context, it is instructive briefly to examine the way these currents address the concept of desire. In Hegel's idealist dialectic of human history (as interpreted, it must be noted, by the key figure in French intellectual history of Alexandre Kojève in lectures at the *École Normale Supérieure* in the 1930s), desire is the means by which human consciousness or self-consciousness emerges and develops out of the passivity of the organic. Because of its physical needs, the organic is not self-sufficient, and while its relationship of lack to an object might lead to self-consciousness, this will fail since the remedying of that lack destroys the sense of lacking something. True self-consciousness can emerge only in a relation with another desiring subject, which acknowledges me without negating itself as a consciousness: a relation of mutual recognition. However, this relation is unstable because of the conflict between a wish for self-sufficiency or self-coincidence, and the need for the other to recognise and reflect me. A solution is for one of the consciousnesses to attempt to create a situation in which it is recognised without having to recognise in return, a struggle for prestige which forms the basis of Hegel's master–slave dialectic and the beginning of history, a history that will culminate in a 'true' concept of self based on reciprocity, unity, and the abandonment of coercion and of aspirations to absolute autonomy. Sartrean Existentialism adapts (among other philosophical traditions) this master–slave dialectic in its portrayal of duels of consciousnesses, with the 'authentic' response that of recognising the Other as an individual liberty rather than falling into the 'bad faith' represented by the positions of both master and slave. In Hegel, then, desire is the way in which consciousness comes to be revealed, with the Other or difference, in one way or another, assimilated to identity. Sartre emphasises the (precarious) self-reflexiveness of consciousness and uses it to develop his notions of political responsibility and commitment. It should be stressed here that while Sartre posits consciousness as ultimately free and not determined, he certainly does not theorise an autonomous ego, for the bulk of his work is devoted to exploring the different constraints in history and society, those *situations* in which it always operates. If, as we have seen, Hocquenghem comes to reject *engagement*,[2] he also recognises the role of Sartre and of his philosophical legacy in the events surrounding the FHAR in 1971.

The 'structuralist' assault on the Hegelianised Marxism/ Existentialism/humanist nexus takes place from the early 1960s via the anthropology of Lévi-Strauss and the rediscovery of the linguistics of Saussure. Here the emphasis is on the ways in which human societies are governed by symbolic systems which rely on relationships of difference. What we might call consciousness or the ego is in fact contingent upon a system of signs, be they language, or myth, and this is the case for all societies, a challenge to the Hegelian or Marxist notions of dialectic and 'progress'. The 'structuralist Marxist' Louis Althusser thus emphasises the 'relative autonomy' of the economic, political and ideological, challenging the classical base/superstructure model, and seeks to rescue the 'scientific' Marx that was the analyst of *Capital* from the 'humanist' heritage of the early writings with their Hegelian notions such as 'alienation'.[3] The focus on the ideological to be found in his seminal 1969 essay 'Ideology and Ideological State Apparatuses'[4] thus stresses the way in which in society we are 'interpellated' as subjects in an 'imaginary relation to the real', so that capitalist society reproduces itself and passes itself off as inevitable. This essay is partly a response to the perceived failure of the May 1968 movement, as

well as an attempt to get the French Communist Party off the hook
for its lack of a revolutionary leadership or goal. What is important
for our purposes is the emphasis here on the meanings capitalist
society throws up, and how those symbolic systems constitute our
identity. Any political project must take account of subjectivity.

It is here that psychoanalysis – and desire – play a role. Indeed,
it was Althusser himself who invited Jacques Lacan to lecture at
the Ecole Normale Supérieure from the early 1960s, and his
concept of the subject is indebted to him. Lacan, heavily influenced
by Hegel in the immediate post-war years, adapts the Saussurean
model of the arbitrary nature of the sign and split between signifier
(the vehicle for meaning) and signified (the 'concept'), as well as
the Freudian notion of the Oedipus complex that involves the
(male) child renouncing the desire for the mother under the threat
of castration, to develop an account of desire, language and identity
which is at complete odds with the Hegel-Sartre tradition, but which
is nonetheless able to give an account of the human subject and
its emergence which is absent from most structuralists' analyses of
systems of meaning. For Lacan, the ego is based on misrecognition, prohibition, and loss. The infant's early life is characterised
by a period of fusion with the maternal body – the Imaginary – when
it cannot differentiate itself or its body parts, and also the famous
'mirror phase' in which it (mis)recognises its representation as full
and unified. The entry into the symbolic order of language and thus
individual subjectivity involves a renunciation of the union with the
mother and an acceptance of the incest taboo and the Law of the
Father, the Phallus – the metaphor for sexual difference – as transcendental presence or lack characteristic of the signifier, as perpetual
third party in the process of signification. The individual desiring
subject is thus split, and continues to seek a plenitude which is irre-
deemably lost.

While this is far from the anxious consciousness of Existentialism,
it is also far from the complacent bourgeois subject confident in
society's norms (such as those of gender and sexuality), in the stability
and unity of his/her identity and capacity for self-reflection. Sherry
Turkle has argued that the events of May 1968 are closely linked
to the psychoanalytic politics that prevailed in left-wing circles
from the 1970s onwards (we recall that in 1979 the MLF became
legally consubstantial with the group *Psych et Po*), in the way in which,
as we have seen, they catalysed the exploration of connections
between the politics and the self:

> they were analogous to attempts to re-create the illusion of
> community where it had disappeared; but in their form of
> expression that denied traditional boundaries between people,

between the private and the public, and between the taboo and the permissible, they looked ahead to something new.[5]

Society inhabits us. The consequences of this realisation, and the central role assigned to it, form one of the main intellectual urgencies of *Le Désir homosexuel*.

However, while the book is about 'social ideology', it is also about 'libidinal energy' and 'the strength of [a] desire'.[6] It is not entitled 'Homosexuality', which, it is made clear, is simply another modality of the 'social ideology'. 'Homosexual' is not a substantive (we recall the misgivings about identity in the previous chapter) but is adjectivally subordinated to 'desire' because for Hocquenghem the importance of 'homosexual desire' is that 'to some extent it reveals the process of the self-production of desire'[7] and 'is in fact a desire for pleasure whatever the system'.[8] One of his starting points is based on Freud's notion of the polymorphous perversity of desire, the way in which in children for example desire is undifferentiated. Criticising the contemporary biologistic notion of homosexuals as belonging to some 'third sex', Freud remarked in 1905:

> The most important perversion [not a value judgement for Freud], homosexuality, hardly deserves the name. It comes down to a general disposition to bisexuality ... All human beings are capable of making a homosexual object-choice and have in fact made one in their unconscious.[9]

How, then, is this fundamental undifferentiated or even bisexual desire organised, split up? Hocquenghem's answer is clear: 'beneath this universalisation of homosexuality in fact lurks the universalisation of the Oedipus complex', which in Freudian theory ensures that 'homosexuals' are 'different yet subject to the same rules'.[10] If, as we shall see, the Freudian and even Lacanian traditions are unsatisfactory for Hocquenghem because they are based on lack (rather than a 'self-producing' 'desire for pleasure'), then what is the basis of his own concept of desire?

If the term 'post-structuralist' is of any usefulness in delineating certain French thinkers and intellectual trends of the 1970s and 1980s, it can be invoked to characterise two sometimes interrelating stances. One is the undermining of any stability or fixity of identity, consciousness, knowledge or truth, primarily through an emphasis on the workings of the linguistic signifier in the domains of philosophy (for example Derrida), history (for example Foucault, as we shall see), society (for example Baudrillard). The other is the emphasis on the cause of that undermining being placed, not so much on lack or absence, but on some kind of positivity beyond or before language. For Hocquenghem in the early 1970s, inspi-

ration lay in to a certain extent Jean-François Lyotard but especially
Gilles Deleuze and Félix Guattari, whose *L'Anti-Oedipe: capitalisme et schizophrénie/Anti-Oedipus: Capitalism and Schizophrenia* was
published in 1972. *Le Désir homosexuel* draws heavily on this work,
and it is necessary to make an extensive detour into it in order to
understand the terms involved and issues at stake. We shall see that
via *L'Anti-Oedipe* Hocquenghem is locking into theoretical traditions
based not on Hegel but on above all Nietzsche.

In *L'Anti-Oedipe*, desire is seen in terms of production, connections
and flows that operate beyond the categories of the personal and
the human: 'man and nature are not like two opposite terms con-
fronting each other ... rather, they are one and the same essential
reality, the producer-product'.[11] The production of desire takes place
through machines, not here a metaphor, but a model of connections and flows that is valid everywhere, in the social and technical
domains as well as the biological. In sex, in manual and intellectual labour, in art, in the weather, desiring machines organise
recurring states of intensity out of potentialities. This is worlds apart
from that Cartesian rational tradition that had by and large characterised French philosophical notions of the self. As Rosi Braidotti
puts it:

> In the classical theory of subjectivity as illustrated by the
> Cartesian cogito, the production of meaning is regulated by the
> relation between those bodies that are defined as capable of action
> and those which are acted upon. The active–reactive distinc-
> tion allows for the two ontological categories of Being and
> non-Being, that is, of the same-as and different-from, whose
> dialectical relationship upholds a single meaning and system of
> representation.[12]

The (individual, human) subject is in contrast here neither a full
consciousness, nor a product of lack or repression as in Freudo-
Lacanian psychoanalysis, but an effect of productive desire: 'an open
series of intensive elements, all of them positive, that are never an
expression of the final equilibrium of the system, but consist,
rather, of an unlimited number of stationary metastable states
through which a subject passes'.[13] If we contrast this view of the
universe with that of one of Deleuze's main philosophical inspira-
tions, Henri Bergson, we might say that what is overcome is the
binary opposition set up between the 'mechanical' and 'life' (clashes
between which are for example central to Bergson's theory of
laughter), but what is retained is the notion of becoming, and of
its unrepresentability, its incompatibility with the spatial. For
example, Bergson's notion that inner time or *la durée* is of a different
realm than the measurements on a clock face is the idealist forebear,

via Deleuze and Guattari, of one of Hocquenghem's formulations
from 1977:

> everything is a certain form of movement, of desire, which is
> then divided and sliced up, isolated in a certain number of
> categories of intellectual activity such as knowledge or politics
> ... every time we enter a movement of abstraction we withdraw
> from this desiring movement, we become immobilised in dead
> shapes, in solidified knowledge.[14]

The libido, then, operates on the level of the fragment, of a process
of bits linking up, of the *molecular*.

However, the desiring machines operate above as well as below
the level of 'the human person', for it is society which at different
points in historical development distributes desire in different ways
through a process of coding, that is of signification which stabilises
desire in patterns. This is the level of the *molar*, that attempt at a
collective level to create a whole, (an image of) unity that, because
of the energy of molecular becomings, is always highly approximate.
Far from the link between sex and social organisation being a
question of sublimation and repression, as in Freud, Deleuze and
Guattari see the socius, that abstract machine of society, as that
which relates desiring production to social production, 'how social
production and relations of production are an institution of desire,
and how affects and drives form part of the infrastructure itself'.[15]
They proceed to trace the molar organisation of desire across three
phases of human history. The first is the territorial machine of
primitive society, in which the earth (*la terre*) is the site of both social
and desiring production. The second is the creation of the (imperial)
state, in which the body of the despot replaces the earth as the point
of convergence of the social and desiring flows, a socius characterised by paranoia and terror. The third is of course capitalism, a
qualitatively different state of affairs, for it is incapable of providing
a globalising, intrinsic code and tends to decode and deterritori-
alise desire (this can be understood, for example, as the way in which
capitalism uproots and sweeps away tradition in a never-ending
process of destabilisation, a factor of modernity we shall discuss
in the next chapter). The abstraction of money is an axiomatic
distinct from previous epochs:

> The organs and agents no longer pass through a coding of
> flows of alliance and filiation, but through an axiomatic of
> decoded flows. Consequently, the capitalist formation of sov-
> ereignty will need an intimate colonial formation that corresponds
> to it, to which it will be applied, and without which it would
> have no hold on the productions of the unconscious.[16]

The formation is that of 'Oedipus'.

For Deleuze and Guattari, the Oedipus complex and the psycho-analytic institution it arises from, are the last territoriality of desire. It is about the representation and not production of desire. The complex marks a disjunction in the connecting flows of desire, assigning us all to fixed and docile units governed by the phallus as it distributes the flows according to the either/or of gender, of having it or not having it, and binds us to a structuring based on infantile family relationships:

> everywhere we encounter the analytic process that consists in extrapolating a transcendent and common something, but that is a common-universal for the sole purpose of introducing lack into desire, in situating and specifying persons and an ego under one aspect or another of its absence, and imposing an exclusive direction on the disjunction of the senses.[17]

The double-bind of Oedipus is that either you integrate or conform, or you become a neurotic. The 'solution' presented in *L'Anti-Oedipe* is that of 'schizo-analysis', for Deleuze and Guattari see in the schizophrenic a rejection of this impasse. The schizophrenic goes beyond the norm, the flows are decoded, deterritorialised, in a manner which represents not revolution, but the potential for revolution.

There are political stakes here, not only for the relationship between 'revolution' and the twentieth-century (notably Soviet) experience, but also for an understanding of gender and sexual politics. First, *L'Anti-Oedipe* is invaluable for the way it seeks to challenge the transhistorical assumptions of conventional psycho-analysis, and to delineate ways of mapping the always mutually dependent relation in history between social and desiring production. Its 'anti-humanism' represents not inhumane relativism but a prob-lematisation of the theoretical assumptions, notably of totalisation, which have characterised post-Enlightenment thought. To this extent, it is part of a general philosophical move in the 1970s. Arguably, its implications for human life are enriching, because of the emphasis on multi-connectedness and pleasure that is absent from the peregrinations of Hegel's consciousness. As Judith Butler writes of Deleuze's *oeuvre*:

> Because distinction is no longer understood as a prerequisite for identity, otherness no longer presents itself as that to be 'labored upon', superseded or conceptualized; rather, difference is the condition for enjoyment, an enhanced sense of pleasure, the acceleration and intensification of the play of forces which constitute what we might call Nietzsche's version of *jouissance*. Once the requirement of discrete identity no longer governs the

subject, difference is less a source of danger than it is a condition of self-enhancement and pleasure.[18]

The problem is one of political and historical agency. Deleuze and Guattari identify certain artistic practices and practitioners (Artaud, D.H. Lawrence, Henry Miller) that embody the flows of decoded desire, as well as the importance for 'anti-psychiatry' (Guattari was a practising analyst at the La Borde clinic) of schizo-analysis. Their distinction between 'unconscious libidinal investment of group or desire' and 'preconscious investment of class or interest' usefully builds on, for example, Wilhelm Reich's theses about the masses *desiring* fascism, and offers a critical method for examining the ways in which liberation and revolutionary movements can be hijacked by paranoid and despotic patterns of desire. (In this way their work is yet another manifestation of the French intelligentsia's settling of scores with the Soviet experience and the French Communist Party.) Their rejection of the castration complex is of obvious benefit to feminist theory,[19] and they even go as far as to argue that the MLF's ultimate goal is the construction of non-Oedipal women.[20] But as with *Psych et Po*, the emphasis is on the aesthetic and ethical rather than on concrete political action or even anything approaching hegemonic change. The significance for gay politics and for *Le Désir homosexuel* is the rejection of any categorisation based on object-choice, which is simply 'a conjunction of flows of life and of society' that a body and person 'intercept, receive and transmit'.[21] 'Homosexuals' are therefore a *subject group*, partaking of 'the unconscious libidinal investment of desire', rather than a *subjected group*, partaking of 'the preconscious investment of class or interest'.[22] No sexual liberation can take place within Oedipal categories. The difficulty for capitalism and its opponents lies in the oscillations between recoding/reterritorialisation and decoding/deterritorialisation inherent in the system, and therefore the undecidability of contemporary dissent, that is in its capacity for appropriation by the system, through the limiting of the flow of decoded desire or even through its transformation into paranoid despotism, but also its potential for 'schizophrenically' destabilising the capitalist axiomatic, testing its limits, forcing it to complicate itself more and more. The heterogeneous (and very historically situated) bunch conjured up in the text of *L'Anti-Oedipe* helps to illustrate this argument, but also the quandaries as far as any praxis is concerned: 'a Chinese on the horizon, a Cuban missile-launcher, an Arab highjacker [sic], a consul kidnapper, a Black Panther, a May '68, or even stoned hippies, angry gays, etc.'.[23]

Before analysing what Hocquenghem makes of all this in *Le Désir homosexuel*, it is necessary to contextualise his theoretical efforts by invoking one more intertext. The political dilemmas produced by

L'Anti-Oedipe are reproduced in the somewhat oxymoronic label given to the legacy of that 'utopian socialist', Charles-Emile Fourier (1772–1837). Unlike his contemporary Saint-Simon, however, who identified the civilisation that emerged from the eighteenth century and the French Revolution with progress, Fourier sees 'civilisation' as an aberration, its rationality a mask for profound historical failure, notably the bourgeois rule of commerce and the subordination of women. Fourier's utopia is characterised by the maximisation of pleasure, the attainment of a life rich in gratified desire, the transformation of work into pleasure: 'happiness is having the greatest number of passions and being able to satisfy them all'.[24] His communities or *phalanstères* are units for cooperative consumption and production in which the basic twelve drives (sexual, but also olfactory) and their varying combinations (precisely 810) are exquisitely associated, matched and satisfied in turn. All sexual preferences are legitimate. The point here is, first, that Fourier bases his concept of humanity not on an integral person or soul but on passions and the endless permutations of their exchange, not unlike the flows of *L'Anti-Oedipe* which are blocked off and divided by capitalism. Unlike Freud but like Deleuze and Guattari, the relationship between desire and society need not be one of sublimation but of fulfilment. In addition, Fourier's extraordinary cosmogony – in which for example planets are seen as androgynous bodies with two sexes, masculine and feminine copulating at north and south poles respectively – is a sign of his notion of libido as vast, cosmic, gigantic:

> desire does not take as its object persons or things, but the entire surroundings that it traverses, the vibrations and flows of every sort to which it is joined, introducing therein breaks and captures – an always nomadic and migrant desire.[25]

As Hocquenghem argued, Fourier represents an interruption in the emergence of modernity, one which did not give rise to a tradition or orthodoxy[26] (the Surrealists did take an interest in him, but they might be said to have recoded the Dadaist movement that preceded them, and their conceptions of desire hardly got beyond heterosexist norms). While his vision has often been mocked, and its contradictions pinpointed (for example he retains the existence of money, as well as of rich and 'poor' – although the latter live above a minimum threshold – thus neglecting the connection between capital and wage labour), it is easy to see how by the late 1960s and early 1970s it was ripe for rediscovery, as it represented a way of reintroducing desire into political debate, and to begin talking about a cultural revolution in the context of the ideological and technical acceleration of modernity. Indeed, Hocquenghem's friend and collaborator René Schérer argues – rather optimistically – in his 1970 edition of Fourier that the utopian elements of the events of May 1968 ('L'Imagination au pouvoir'/'Imagination to power') corresponded to much of Fourier's vision, with the architecture, encounters and activities of the occupied Sorbonne reminiscent of a *phalanstère*.[27]

Le Désir homosexuel is therefore not about object-choice but about the polymorphousness of desire and the various ways in which the molar seeks to limit molecular flows. Hocquenghem's first strategy is to critique in these terms what we would now call society's homophobia, beginning with the category of paranoia, which demonstrates the way in which homosexual desire is at the centre of society's 'waking dreams'[28] even as, or because, it upsets its codes. The paranoia expressed by society against homosexuals (manifested in its legal and medical dispositions) tended to be mirrored in mainstream 1950s' and 1960s' psychiatry's view that homosexuals were often paranoid, that they were both neurotics and paranoid. Hocquenghem reverses this analysis by returning to Freud. To begin with, Freud saw neurosis as a patient's attempt to disavow 'perversion' (understood in the neutral and descriptive sense of those pleasure-seeking drives outside the category of genital heterosexuality). More importantly, Freud's writings on paranoia show that it tends to be based on the disavowal of homosexuality. Like Deleuze and Guattari, Hocquenghem takes a close interest in the Schreber case, on which Freud based a study of paranoia.[29] Daniel Schreber was a judge in eastern Germany whose *Memoirs of a Nerve Patient* were published in 1913. Schreber's delusional system had him believing he had a mission to redeem the world but only if he were transformed from a man into a woman. His body became the site of miracles, in which he communicated with the natural world. Freud's interpretation of the illness was that it was a defensive strategy based on the outburst of a homosexual impulse, since 'Generally speaking, every human being oscillates all through his life between heterosexual and homosexual feelings, and any frustration or disappointment in the one direction is apt to drive him over into the other.'[30] The object of these feelings was Flechsig, his physician, surrogate for his dead father and older brother. The sun that 'conversed' with Schreber symbolised the father, and the delusion of becoming a woman represented a way of dealing with the castration threat as wishful fantasy. Hocquenghem thus uses this case to demonstrate that 'anti-homosexual paranoia' in society is based on that society's mechanisms of desire and disavowal which reproduce the heterosexual norm. Schreber's feelings of guilt are turned into the grandeur of being the world's redeemer, his (homosexual) desire can be experienced only as sacrifice.

However, Hocquenghem's understanding of the reproduction of those norms begins at the point where he departs from Freud. As he says, Schreber can deal with his homosexual desire only as a woman, and therefore, in classical Freudian terms, castrated by the father. Moreover, that figure of 'woman' is organised as 'either a goddess or charwoman, an archetype or a sexual object. Schreber experiences homosexuality as a heterosexual would imagine it to be experienced.'[31] This is because the terms of Freud's analysis are those of Oedipus, a system whose domination of the polymorphousness of desire begins with the category of narcissism, closely linked to paranoia. For Freud, narcissism is between auto-erotism and object-love, as the child first unifies its polymorphous desire through a desiring relationship with its own body. It then turns to an external object with similar genitals, and then in most cases to heterosexual objects. Those adults manifestly homosexual have thus not reached the latter stage. The rest retain homosexual tendencies, but these are by and large sublimated, that is, combined with portions of the ego-instincts, 'thus contributing an erotic factor to friendship and comradeship, to *esprit de corps* and to the love of mankind in general'.[32] There is always, however, a danger of regression, and in paranoics there is a fixation at the stage of narcissism, a step back from sublimated homosexuality, which is why paranoia is about a defensive strategy against homosexual desires.

Clearly, this interpretation of the organisation of desire is completely unacceptable to Hocquenghem. (Indeed, Deleuze and Guattari see in Schreber not the segregations of paranoia, but the schizophrenia of radical decoding: thus the sun is not a symbol of his father but part of a Fourier-like cosmology of desire.) Narcissism is indeed a knot of desire which looks backwards and forwards, 'the end of the unconsciousness of non-human sex, and the beginning of personalised and imaginary Oedipal sexuality'.[33] In fact, the very notion of object-choice, be it homosexual or heterosexual, presupposes a bodily unity integrating the drives, and the entry into a system of binaries, of the similar and different. Moreover, that unity can be imposed only *retrospectively*, as a fiction subsequent to the Lacanian mirror stage. Homosexual object-choice is thus a matter of entering a binary system suffused with guilt because homosexual *desire* is otherwise sublimated and is a source of social anxiety, or to put it another way, 'sublimation is simply homosexuality in its historical family truth'.[34] Homosexual desire is thus a crack in the system, and points back to polymorphousness.

What is crucial here for Hocquenghem is that this narrative of desire is a creation of the molar, of the social order, including the psychoanalytic institution. It produces neurotic, guilt-ridden, 'Oedipalised' individuals, for whom homosexual desire can be legitimately experienced only as sublimation or abjection. It is thus possible to be an Oedipalised homosexual, whether for example in turn-of-the-century 'third sex' or even later chromosomal theories, when the *difference* of the homosexual is matched by the *similarity* of 'a role which safeguards the discriminating value of the penis, without which one could simply cast him as a woman'.[35] And while Freud attacked third sex theories, the categories of Oedipus act in analogous ways to ensure that, while homosexuals may be different, they abide by similar rules of identity, sexual difference and lack. This can reach the point where, for example, homosexual men can be perceived as 'lacking' the essential object of desire, as hating women (posited here as lack in an Oedipal system which sees them as lacking).

This widespread Oedipalisation is due to the crisis of the social institutions of capitalism, and represents the system's best bet for stemming the decoding of flows and desire. What counter-strategies are proposed in *Le Désir homosexuel*? One is the rehabilitation of *la drague* or 'promiscuous' homosexual cruising, 'the system in which polyvocal desire is plugged in on a non-exclusive basis', where 'everything is possible at any moment: organs look for each other and plug in, unaware of the law of exclusive disjunction'.[36] This is analogous to Deleuze and Guattari's notions of the 'voyaging schizophrenic' poised for desire, and of the 'aleatory relations' which for example in art can creatively link radically distinct elements.[37] Another counter-strategy is one based on the sexuality of minors.[38] But the most sustained discussion is to be found in perhaps the strongest section of *Le Désir homosexuel*, in which Hocquenghem promotes the deprivatisation of the anus.[39]

This is linked to a passage in *L'Anti-Oedipe* where Deleuze and Guattari discuss the nature of despotic rule. The signifying system of such a regime is based on the intensely desiring body of the despot, a plenum upon which all of society's organs are inscribed, that is, derive their meaning via the mediations of state administration. If the plenitude of that body is symbolically broken, the rule of the despot is ended, his organs detached and scattered. The only surviving memory of what was once the highest body is of the lowest organ, the anus, and it is this organ which in the codes of capitalism is symbolically ostracised, socially bereft.[40] The signifying organ *par excellence* in capitalist society is of course the phallus, distributing the codes of sexual difference, Oedipalised personhood, and hierarchy, 'dividing human beings into people who are afraid of losing their penis and people who wish they had one'.[41]

The attempted reterritorialisations of capitalism are able to address 'homosexuality' by placing it in the sphere of sublimation and Oedipal guilt, where at best 'homosexuals' are 'failed "normal people"', their desire, apart from their object-choice, enclosed within the same rules as everyone else. Since Hocquenghem rejects this, the obvious place to go from the heights of the sublime is 'the abyss of non-personalised and uncodified desire'. Whereas the phallus is profoundly social, the anus – to be distinguished of course from the buttocks – is private, devoid of any signification other than in sublimation, whether in the classically 'anal' personality devoted to order, or in money, or in the whole notion of the 'private person', since it is the most private organ of all and thus 'enables the division between society and the individual to be made'. (The phallus is of course to be distinguished from the penis, which is private, although its forbidden exposure relates back to the great social signifier.) The child's apprenticeship in anal cleanliness (*propreté* in French) is linked to its acquisition of responsible personhood and thus private property (*propriété*). Not to hold back 'is to risk joining up, through the flux of excrement, with the non-differentiation of desire'. It is the phallus which distributes gender and identity, whereas sexual difference is not predicated on the view from behind.

In this way, the anus as site of symbolic meaning is incompatible with any castration threat – 'No one ever threatens to take away your anus' – and its release into desiring activity would undermine the 'jealousy-competition' system, particularly between men, predicated on the phallus (a notion that reconnects with the connection between homophobia and paranoia). Reversing the Freudian scenario which surpasses the component drives of orality and anality in favour of genitality, Hocquenghem argues that what is necessary is detachment from the phallus in favour of the anus. This would bring about 'the collapse of both the sublimating phallic hierarchy and the individual/society double-bind'.

Hocquenghem's argument connects not so much with psychoanalytic and philosophical tradition but with the notion of the carnivalesque body undermining hierarchy, separation and unity developed by Mikhail Bakhtin's study of market-place culture in *Rabelais and His World*, although he does not acknowledge this. The provocative nature of this section of *Le Désir homosexuel* is echoed in the undoubted humour of his style, in which 'high' notions of the serious are subverted. However, it is unclear precisely whose desire is in play. On the one hand, 'The desiring use of the anus made by homosexuals is the chief, if not the exclusive one.' On the other, 'Homosexuality is always connected with the anus, even though – as Kinsey's precious statistics demonstrate[42] – anal intercourse is still the exception even among homosexuals.' His attempt to distinguish between polymorphous 'homosexual desire' and Oedipalised 'homosexuality' is undermined by such slippages. And if he is interested in 'homosexuality' as a 'relation of desire' rather than as 'an ontological standpoint',[43] then we might well ask who are the 'homosexuals' he keeps talking about. It is in this way that his theories are at their most utopian. Similar inconsistencies can be traced in his use of the term 'nature'. On the one hand, arguments from nature, be they pro-homosexuality as in Gide or anti- as in the French penal code, are all complicit in a regression to paranoic territorialisations existing before the bourgeois revolution based its law on 'reason'.[44] On the other, 'nature' can become 'a term of equivalence with the immediacy of desire'[45] (over-simplified critiques of Deleuze and Guattari have certainly accused them of 'naturalism' in *L'Anti-Oedipe*).

The way forward clearly lies neither with liberalism nor the bureaucratised Communist Party. Hocquenghem's approach builds on, but gets beyond, that of both Reich and Marcuse, the most influential synthesisers of Marx and Freud in the debates of the 1960s: Reich's discussions of a revolution and sexuality are discredited because of his heterosexism, whereas Marcuse's formulation of the 'repressive desublimations' prevalent in consumer society are reworked in the terms of *L'Anti-Oedipe* as reterritorialisations of decoded flows in capitalism, with the emphasis on exploring ways of desublimating non-repressively by letting desire flow. The importance of the FHAR in this theoretical vocabulary is not to become an agent of reterritorialisation – even the notion of 'gay pride' falls within the Oedipal system[46] – but to work on the level of the molecular, 'Homosexual action, not action in favour of homosexuality.'[47] By redefining what is central and marginal to revolutionary activity, by in fact abolishing the centre, the gay movement 'contradicts the system of political thought'[48] in a struggle against 'this civilisation's imaginary affective system'.[49] This kind of discourse is to be judged as part of the cultural field emerging out of May 1968 and interacting with the changed political and social landscape of the 1980s.

Jeffrey Weeks's very useful preface to the 1978 edition of the English translation of *Le Désir homosexuel* (reproduced in the 1993 version) touches on some of the above points and develops others. While I would question the notion that Hocquenghem's analysis of anti-homosexual paranoia is dependent upon a hydraulic theory of sexuality in which expression in one place is compensated for by sublimation somewhere else (for Hocquenghem, it is a question of mechanisms for disavowing and channelling the flows of unquantifiable desire), it is certainly the case that Hocquenghem seems unable to account for, not only the emergence of gay individuals, but also gay social and historical identities. His neglect of lesbianism explicitly is in part compensated for by the implications for trans- or even post-gender theories that by-pass the phallus (we recall his contemporaneity with not only *L'Anti-Oedipe* but also the emerging 'New French Feminisms'). And while the place and categorisation

of 'sodomy' is a major historical issue, we were reminded in Britain
of the cultural resonances of anal sex during the House of Commons
debate on the age of consent in February 1994, notably in a speech
by the late Nicholas Fairbairn MP.[50]

The distinctiveness of Hocquenghem's theoretical position in 1972
is underlined if we compare the arguments of *Le Désir homosexuel*
to those of that other 1970s' theoretical text of gay liberation,
Mario Mieli's *Homosexuality and Liberation*, first published in Italy
in 1977. Like Hocquenghem, Mieli starts from the idea of the polymorphousness of desire. The emergence of gay identity politics in
the 1970s is a means to an end, that end being the liberation of
Eros and of 'trans-sexualism'. He opposes 'integration' into this
society and economy. This positions him against traditional theses
on the left, since he argues that desire is part of the base not super-
structure:[51] the economy (rather than, in Hocquenghem, the
prevailing regime of desire and identity) is dependent on sublimation.
Sceptical of the psychoanalytic institution, he argues for promis-
cuity against exclusiveness, the radical potential of schizophrenia,[52]
and for the fact of 'our bodily being-in-becoming'.[53] However, the
grid of analysis differs. Whereas Hocquenghem sees anti-homosexual
paranoia and Oedipalisation as facts of desire organised and
channelled in a certain way, Mieli believes there is something else
outside which represses Eros, and that is ideology,[54] a concept
Deleuze and Guattari, for example, explicitly reject. Mieli's concept
of Eros is therefore grounded not only in Freudian theory but in
Jung's trans-historical archetypes, and, like Gide in *Corydon*, from
'nature'. He endearingly informs the reader that there are gay
ducks.[55] More importantly, science, notably genetics and embryo
research, is invoked to emphasise the fundamental hermaphrodism
of every human being.

This is the basis of Mieli's far more sustained engagement with
'the feminine': 'one of the greatest disasters that has happened to
our species: the refusal by the man to recognise the "woman" in
himself, i.e. to recognise his trans-sexuality'.[56] Whereas
Hocquenghem emphasises undifferentiated desire, Mieli is interested
in the concepts of 'humanity' and 'the person', and their radical
erotic and ethical amelioration. The valorisation of anal eroticism,
and even the concept of the 'trans-sexual', are important not for
the flows of desire but for the breakdown of the society's gender
system in favour of women: 'homosexual men who get fucked are
closer to trans-sexuality, and tend to overcome the polarity between
the sexes'.[57] Heterosexual men, since part of their Eros is sublimated,
impose an alienated auto-eroticism on women, and Mieli argues
that it is women and gay men who are capable of and should aspire
to full erotic relations. Mieli thus deploys typically modernist
notions of authenticity, alienation and reification which enable

him to talk about '*genuine* loving desire'.[58] (Needless to say, the death of Pasolini is thus seen in very different terms from Hocquenghem: for Mieli, the murdering hustler *conformed* to the structures of heterosexual society.)[59] If 'love' gets us beyond individualism and solipsism, and has 'the tendency to annihilate the outworn neurotic and ego-istic categories of "subject" and "object"', it is from the point of view of a Hegelian reconciliation at the end of a dialectic of alienation. This vocabulary occurs frequently in *Homosexuality and Liberation*: the gay and feminist movements are the antithesis of institutionalised normality;[60] the liberation of Eros will mean 'releasing our aesthetic and communist potential, our desire for community and for pleasure that has grown latently over the millenia [sic]'.[61] (The novel definition of 'communism' is 'the rediscovery of bodies and their fundamental communicative function, their polymorphous potential for love'.)[62] Mieli's opposition to the commercial gay scene, or 'the programme of commercialisation and exploitation of homosexuality on the part of capitalist enterprise', is based not so much on the way it creates new, fixed, docile subjects out of undifferentiated desire, but on the way it actually prevents the emergence or expression of authentic consciousnesses. Mieli is here drawing heavily on Herbert Marcuse's analysis of consumer society, *One-Dimensional Man*, and the concept of repressive desublimation, in which the alienating reifications of commodified capitalism are distorting the consciousnesses and pleasures to be found in 'permissive', consumer societies. Mieli is at pains, however, to argue that the grounding of his discourse in such vocabulary does not imply an inert humanism, but rather a notion of becoming.[63]

Mieli's work also throws up some crucial questions regarding desire and history, or desire in history. For example, the account of the treatment of 'homosexuals' in the Roman Empire to be found in Chapter Three, 'Fire and Brimstone, or How Homosexuals Became Gay', implies the persistence across different epochs of a stable category of people defined by their same-sex desire. Contemporary 'gay' identity is simply the self-conscious political and emancipatory expression of that identity. In a way, this echoes Mieli's confidence in his use of the by implication trans-historical critical categories of 'genuine', 'alienated' (from what essence?) and so on. So while his summary in the chapter is historical, it is not historicist in the sense of examining the different and changing discourses in any given period which might map out questions of sexuality, identity and truth. The path history takes is not, as it were, a straight one. Hocquenghem in *Le Désir homosexuel* does acknowledge, via Michel Foucault's *Histoire de la folie à l'âge classique/Madness and Civilisation* of 1961, that it is societies in history which create 'means for classifying the unclassifiable',[64] be they mental hospitals for the insane, or the category 'homosexual' for persons engaging in same-sex acts. However, although Hocquenghem does assert that 'The establishment of homosexuality as a separate category goes hand in hand with its repression',[65] this is subordinated in that text to the arguments about Oedipalisation and the broad historical structurings of desire mapped out in *L'Anti-Oedipe*: 'Savages, Barbarians, Civilised Men'.

By the late 1970s however, the profound mutations in 'homosexual' lives and culture occurring in the Western world were prompting more sustained reflections on the relations between desire and historical change. (It is here of course that we must retrospectively problematise my use so far in this study of the terms 'homosexual', 'gay' and *pédé* as all representing historically contingent ways of mapping out desire.) The impetus behind these reflections were matched by Michel Foucault's historical and theoretical work on the prison (*Surveiller et punir/Discipline and Punish*, 1975) and sexuality (*Histoire de la sexualité, vol. 1/History of Sexuality*, 1976). Foucault's emphasis is on the way in which power as discourse organises our thinking about 'oppression' and identity. This means an abandonment of the 'repressive hypothesis' (exemplified by Mieli), which has argued that there is something 'natural' or at least beyond discourse which the apparatuses of authority and society then distort, damage, or seek to suppress. On the contrary, it is discourse which in a positive sense gives rise to our sexual categories, our understanding of ourselves as sexual beings. Thus, for example, from the role of the Catholic confession onwards, even and especially at the height of the Victorian era, sex is constantly talked about rather than passed over in silence. In the modern era, this results in the crucial change from discourse about acts to discourse about identity. Whereas the principle category for mapping out same-sex desire before the mid-nineteenth century was that of 'sodomy' – an act which theoretically anyone could indulge in, and one which could extend to any kind of non-reproductive sex – from the 1860s the 'scientific-rational' term 'homosexual' came to refer to a *species* of person. One result of this was that many interpellated by such a designation appropriated that identity both politically and culturally, hence the homosexual rights movements active particularly in Germany at the turn of the century, the origin of our contemporary 'gay' movements. But this can also be seen as part of a general Enlightenment phenomenon in which social order is achieved not through external coercion but through internalised processes, a self-surveillance the model and metaphor for which is the panopticon in prison architecture, in which every cell and prisoner is visible from a central point. We are always being watched. Foucault, ultimately more sympathetic to pre-Enlightenment heterogeneities, thus enables us historically to relativise identities and sexualities in a more precise way than the broad description of cultural codings and decodings in *L'Anti-Oedipe*.

In *La Dérive homosexuelle* of 1977, Hocquenghem's misgivings about the commercialisation and *embourgeoisement* of homosexuality are expressed in very Foucauldian terms. Rather than representing a straightforward liberation or desublimation, the changes of the 1970s are seen as part of a redistribution of terms and categories within, rather than beyond, the workings of power. The gay movement can be read as the avant-garde of the new sexual arrangements. For example, 'coming out' in the early 1970s, reminiscent of the role of Catholic confession in earlier times, announces a process through which by the end of the decade the whole society is talking incessantly about sex and its link with truth and personal identity. The expected 'liberalisation' of anti-homosexual legislation will be matched by a tightening of the apparatus elsewhere, as regards children's sexuality, public sex, sexological/medical orthodoxies, and the demise of those heterogeneities of inter-class sex or drag (*les folles*) which formerly characterised the homosexual subculture. (This is the theoretical context for his opposition to feminist puritanism we looked at in the previous chapter.)

> Since the right to 'private life' that is coming is no longer grounded in Nature or God, it will tend to become a huge system of compensations between sub-groups, defined by the risks they run and make others run. Sex will no longer be the great enemy, but a sector to talk about clearly, an anarchy to sort out and impose order upon thanks to the new sexological enlightenment. Homosexuals will have to pay for their new 'recognition' with the sacrifice of their own margins and their own irrationalities.[66]

Hocquenghem argues that, similarly, the often *ad hoc* 'anti-homosexual' legislation in the French penal code was used in an exploratory way, and was eventually used against transvestites. 'Homosexual politics' in the 1970s meant accepting an interpellation and walking into a trap of post-Enlightenment power. The gay movement founded a new normality and Law, even invoking republicanism to criticise the archaisms of the penal code's reference to nature and implications of Christian morality. The rationalisation of the Law is not a straightforward 'progress', but an opportunity for the system to use dissent for its own ends, that of renewal, reformulation, fine-tuning. Society will put up with the homosexual rather than seek to get rid of him, but only by distinguishing between 'good' and 'bad' practices and preventing any disruptions to the dominant order (Hocquenghem is thinking notably of society's segregation of children).

This focus on history that characterised the late 1970s has its apogee in the book and film of 1979, *Race d'Ep! Un Siècle d'images de l'homosexualité* ('*rasdep*' is back-slang for *pédéraste*). This chronicle of images and identities of homosexuality creates a striking narrative, as when twentieth-century history is read in terms of the emerging homosexual identity and movement flourishing in Europe between 1920 and 1933, only to be destroyed almost simultaneously by Nazism and Stalinism. The setback of this bloody interruption explains the delay until the late 1960s and the young adulthood of the post-war generation before a new movement could emerge. However, *Race d'Ep* also succeeds in completely deconstructing its subject, for it makes clear that 'homosexuality' and 'the homosexual' are ephemeral categories, provisional solutions to the dilemmas of modernity. While same-sex desire has always existed, homosexual identity has not, so 'gay liberation' is certainly not the culmination of 'a gradual and invincible process founded on the progressive bringing to light of a pre-existing and irrepressible reality'. The most imaginary of all minority modes of being, it is the least rooted in an essence or nature.[67]

This is not to say that gay political struggle is not worth waging. Hocquenghem is pointing out, however, that it is never a straight-forward question of more freedom *or* more repression, that it is always a two-way street, and any gay politics must be vigilant of that if its goal is going to be a wider social liberation rather than simply an accommodation to the normalcy of 'rights'. Moreover, the question of history raises that of historical periodisation on the cusp of the 1970s and 1980s, and the profound social, technological and political change which was rewriting the agendas of French society and the Western world in general. The move to history, accompanied by a disinvestment in traditional political struggle, and, for Hocquenghem, even to an extent post-traditional struggle, went hand in hand for many French thinkers with a move to ethics and aesthetics. Lyotard's *La Condition postmoderne/The Postmodern Condition* of 1979 corresponds to both operations, in its periodisation and also in its attempt to find resistant ways of dealing with the crisis of truth claims and of the legitimacy of knowledge in a world system in which knowledge had become commodified. Michel Foucault's diagnoses of modernity would lead him in the second and third volumes of *Histoire de la sexualité*, published in 1984, to explore the alternative mappings of the sexual to be found in the ethical structures of ancient Greece and Rome. Even in the preface to the American edition of *L'Anti-Oedipe* in 1977, Foucault had stressed the ethical dimension of Deleuze and Guattari's work, an introduction to non-fascist life based on deindividualisation, since 'the individual is the product of power'.[68] (The liberal moralism of Glucksmann and Lévy can be seen as the caricatured version of this return to the ethical.)

Hocquenghem was aware that, as well as revealing diverse pasts, history also allows us to speak of possible futures. In the development of modernity over the past twenty years which some have called post-modernity, what possibilities and what impediments exist for desire? The discourse of Mario Mieli allows a political and historical purchase on the process of commodification:

> The logic of money and profit that determines the liberalisation of the so-called 'perversions' is not simply an economic fact; it promotes the submission to capital of the whole of human life.
>
> This demonstrates the very complex task of our revolutionary project, to recognise and express a humanity that transcends capital, without offering ourselves up to be devoured by it. In fact, if this should happen, then capital would simply vomit us up again in its own forms, with a view to making use of us to reproduce a new 'humanity', even more programmable, because already programmed in advance.[69]

Hocquenghem is haunted, not only by capitalism's all-pervasiveness, but also by the fact that the politics and even the theories that he has espoused have been so appropriated by the system. We saw at the end of the previous chapter the ambiguous relationship between the 'transversal' and capitalism. Even in 1977, when he is proposing a resistant 'plural perversity', he is at pains to point out that 'the free rein given to these thousands of partial drives, atoms, tiny pluggings-in, Brownian movement of productive desire'[70] represents not the process of capitalist dehumanisation, but a strategy of getting beyond it. The relationships between modernity, post-modernity, desire and identity, and the strategies for resistance that might be historically possible, are the subject of the next chapter.

3

Modernity

The first half of *Comment nous appelez-vous déjà? Ces hommes que l'on dit homosexuels*, published in 1977, is an essay, 'Vivre à midi'/'To Live at Midday', written by the novelist Jean-Louis Bory. Although he refuses both the illusions of 'tolerance' and the aim of integration of homosexuals into the social status quo, he is nonetheless at pains to open a homosexual politics out to the culture of the left from which it has been excluded. The basis of this dialogue is adumbrated in his text, as he seeks to elicit empathy from the implied heterosexual reader through autobiographical representation, and also through analysis and explanation of certain myths about homosexuals. This includes cruising (*la drague*), which has its joys and aesthetics, but which is also 'justified' by the hostility of the surrounding society, which encourages the 'instability and dispersion' of homosexual acts. In any case, Bory is quick to affirm, many homosexuals have long-term relationships.[1] In a discourse familiar since the 1970s, Bory straightforwardly locates the transformation of the social status of homosexuals in a renewed humanist project, the creation of 'complete man, including sex': 'It is against the mechanisation and robotisation of man that individual fulfilment through (among other means) sexual freedom will be the indispensable formula for happiness.'[2] At the same time, his method and procedure in this text reproduce that confidence in the whole person or consciousness rationally engaging in a process of education, enlightenment, *bildung*. The title, 'Vivre à midi', suggests the desire and right of homosexuals to participate in the light of day, that is not just in the open but also as part of a wider progressive Enlightenment project.

In stark contrast, Hocquenghem's contribution to this volume, a short story entitled *Oiseau de la nuit/Nightbird*, employs a different mode of address and is a vehicle for quite different reflections on 'progress' and the place within it of 'the homosexual'. The married, middle-class and 'heterosexual' narrator, *'Moi'*/'Me', at some unspecified point of crisis in his life, encounters late at night in a mixed Paris gay café his interlocutor, *'Lui'*/'Him'. The latter, half seductively, half to enable a flow of discourse about sexuality and the self, plies him with drink, fills him in on the stories of the various marginals assembled there, and leads him on a sexual *promenade* through the Parisian night, culminating in the cruising grounds of the Tuileries gardens and the banks of the Seine. The two part after their chaste but revealing encounter, but a brief coda places them in the downstairs toilets of another café, with *Lui* making what turns out to be a humiliating pass at *Moi* without at first realising his identity. *Moi* makes off for his home in the suburbs.

Night for day, determined and defiant marginality instead of humanist fulfilment. Although the dialogue with *Lui* is an 'education' for *Moi*, it is not part of a personal growth, still less the catalyst for sexual experimentation. The sexual underworld is and remains Other to his social and even subject position, and this is explained in terms not of identity but history. To this extent, we are in territory familiar from Hocquenghem's writings of the late 1970s and the refusal of fixed gay identities structured by liberalism and con-sumerism. *Lui* is at pains to emphasise the difference between the fauna of the café and the milieu of the expensive gay clubs of the nearby rue Sainte-Anne, where *Moi* would no doubt encounter colleagues and acquaintances and their now familiarly anathema-tised lifestyle of after-shave and moustaches. The point is that *Moi* and his kind would never enter such a place by accident. The café, however, is non-segregationist, whether between heteros or homos, or in terms of race and class. *Lui* despises 'the levelling-down of progressivism', and is fascinated by 'manias and trash'.[3] This taste for delinquency is thus another example of that plea for heterogeneity in the face of the rationalisations of Enlightenment categories.

The 'modern' and 'modernity' are similarly in play in the relation between *Oiseau de la nuit* and its major intertext, acknowledged on the final page of the afterword to the volume, Diderot's *Le Neveu de Rameau/Rameau's Nephew*. This comparison not only works metonymically – the philosophical dialogues in both works take place as the two pairs of *Moi* and *Lui* wander contiguous Parisian streets – but also structurally. In both works, *Moi* – the middle-class executive or the Diderot figure – is the self that is integrated into the internalised hegemony of social norms. *Lui* – the cruising homosexual or Rameau's nephew – challenges and disrupts those norms, be they the categories of vice and virtue, beauty and ugliness, or sincerity and authenticity. *Lui* in both works is a social performer, flatterer and parasite. The resonances of *Le Neveu de Rameau* for the understanding of our modern period it in part inaugurates have been many: the nephew as *id* to 'Diderot''s *ego*; the Nietzschean 'beyond good and evil'; more intricately, Hegel's fascination in the *Phenomenology of Mind* for the nephew's alienation, and the way in which his self-estrangement marks a necessary stage in the devel-opment of spirit, a necessary detachment from the imposed conditions of the external power of society. Disintegration is necessary for the higher stage of (re-)integration to come beyond

the *ancien régime*.[4] In parallel fashion, *Oiseau de la nuit* is the
id/Nephew to the *ego*/'Diderot' of Bory's *Vivre à midi*, as it introduces
a fissure in its more totalising discourse.

It is inappropriate to impose a Hegelian reading on *Oiseau de la
nuit*, not least because no dialectic is discernible that leads *Lui*'s
musings on sex and identity to some future reconciliation. However,
I wish to stay with these interlocking notions of modernity and 'the
bad side' (which may turn out to be 'good') of society, and link
them to the prevailing aestheticism of the work. The invocation of
Nietzsche underlines one dimension of this. Just as *Lui*, in his
defence of anonymous sex, insists that 'making love' and 'identi-
fying' are two separate actions, so for Nietzsche consciousness
and inwardness impoverish the real, there is nothing beyond
'appearances' (unlike of course for Hegel), and the life force or will
to power, as sensuous surface, is indifferent to 'value'. This world
bereft of grounded values and morality also provides the opportunity for aesthetic delight. Sex for *Lui* is partly about 'free invention',
living aesthetically.[5]

Just as in Nietzsche, 'value' is smuggled back into *Oiseau de la
nuit* via the aesthetic, and, importantly, this aesthetic is materially
and historically grounded in the city, in Paris, in, especially, the
nineteenth-century urban. Helped by alcohol, from the outset *Moi*
realises he is embarking on an aesthetic experience, as the seemingly
ordinary café now seems 'rich with a revitalised urban poetry, the
natural place of nocturnal extravagance'.[6] Just as for *Lui* the 'real'
of pornography is in the unexpected and improbable nature of the
encounters, so urban cruising is about shock and surprise: 'the
catalytic lightning flash between distant poles',[7] 'the movement that
is oblique, underside, surprising, because it eroticises a situation
illicitly withdrawn from its ordinary function'.[8] These encounters
operate '*percées* [breaks, gaps, openings] in the social tissue'.[9] The
urban landscape is crucial to this process, as the encounters are
sought in the *parcours*[10] of Haussmann's Paris, and consummated
amidst that decor – the arcades of the rue de Rivoli, the lamps, the
statues of the Tuileries, the *pissoirs*. This provides the setting for
the 'miraculous' to surge forth against the 'prosaic'. The aesthetic
manifests itself when the convoluted movements and choreogra-
phies of cruising men become a baroque disruption of classical order
in the Tuileries, and when the scene becomes allegorised, the men
as insects, rats, dogs, birds (nightbirds ...), spectres, unicorns.[11]

For *Moi*, the experience leads to the conclusion that all this
marginality is itself a part of the system of social hygiene, 'indispensable to the maintenance of general equilibrium', giving shape
to and isolating the passions of the 'normal'.[12] There is certainly
an ironic reading of this, in that *Moi* has clearly been fascinated by

the whole process, and his attempt at 'othering' only suggests that the Other, as always, is also within. In fact he gives the game away in the next sentence by describing *Lui*'s life as a 'Faustian pact'. What figure more than Faust has come to represent the situation of modern man, making pacts with his passions and with technology as he turns away from the divine to embrace the good and the bad side of development?[13] *Moi* thus has his own Faustian pact, or partakes in that of the West in general. However, the ambiguity of *Oiseau de la nuit* is there: how does *Lui* and what he represents relate to contemporary society, and to the history of that society, notably the avatar of the nineteenth-century city? *Lui* seems to acknowledge he and his kind belong to a past time, to an ephemeral phenomenon of modernity: 'Perhaps we are the last witnesses of customs that will have lasted just a century or two, from the first street-lamp or first *pissotière* to sex education';[14] 'our damned past is worth all normalised futures'.[15] On the other hand, the 'revitalised urban poetry' recognised by *Moi* at the outset manifests itself in the most unpropitious circumstances, for the café decor is as homogenised and 'inauthentic' as anywhere. Significantly however, this 'new' style of decor, which everyone seemed to condemn when it appeared, is now not only accepted – that is, it has become hegemonised, part of the everyday, even a tradition – but able to generate aesthetic experiences, and this is not just because of the presence of *Lui* and his kind. The sexual marginals of *Oiseau de la nuit* belong to a tradition, but as *Lui* points out, that tradition had a beginning. What therefore is the relationship between social and historical change and the emergence of, not only identities, but also aesthetic experiences? What identities and aesthetic experiences are available to us in contemporary society, and what is the relationship between our moment and the previous epoch? Is it a question of the 'modern' and the 'post-modern', and when did one begin and the other end? Why is the aesthetic being privileged, and what are the implications of the term?

To answer these questions, it will be necessary to explore Hocquenghem's theoretical writings of the 1980s. First, however, light can be shone on the meaning of modernity and its relationship with the aesthetic, as well as on the 'poetic' traditions invoked by Hocquenghem, by looking at the work of Walter Benjamin and in particular his writings on Baudelaire and Paris, which in fact form the second major intertext of *Oiseau de la nuit*. Marshall Berman in his penetrating study of modernity reminds us that the latter is always to be understood as a dialectical interrelation between forces of construction and development, and forces of destruction and oppression; between an abundance of possibilities and an emptiness of values; between feelings of merger with and alienation from the modern city. The great modernists of the nineteenth century – and Baudelaire is a prime exemplar – 'all attack this environment passionately, and strive to tear it down or explode it from within; yet all find themselves remarkably at home in it, alive to its possibilities, affirmative even in their radical negations, playful and ironic even in their moments of gravest seriousness and depth'.[16] The twentieth century, however, has tended to sunder these two attitudes. The poems and prose poems of Baudelaire, created at the time of the dramatic transformations wrought by Haussmann during the Second Empire, are often vehicles for primal modern scenes. For example, the sonnet 'À une passante' describes the fleeting encounter with a 'fugitive beauty', the crowd of the boulevard yielding up a figure of fascination that it then swallows up again, 'love', as Benjamin puts it, 'not at first sight, but at last sight'.[17] The construction of the boulevards over the old defensive walls created an innovative environment, 'a new private and public world', a way of being 'private in public'.[18] At the same time, of course, these joys and pleasures have their dark side of increased class polarisation and homelessness provoked by the demolitions. Berman argues that, for example, Baudelaire's prose poem 'Perte d'auréole' crystallises a key moment when the poetry of the modern era finds its source not in purity and spirituality, but in the ugly, the degraded, in filth. This is consistent with the tendency of modern culture to desanctification.

Now for that other emerging category of modernity, the 'homosexual', the new urban experience is consistently lived not simply in a dark, hidden side, but in a wholly intensified manner, and it survives longer. The homelessness and deterritorialisation of capitalist society are redoubled, but territories are staked out. For *Lui* in *Oiseau de la nuit*, the nocturnal urban landscape is a shifting, mobile, kaleidoscopic 'home': one cannot imagine him anywhere else, not for him the socially segmented world of the twentieth-century suburban highway and the 'home' that *Moi* is returning to at the end in a mixture of panic and reluctance. Ironically, *Moi* resanctifies the cruising homosexuals: 'The vaporous globes of the lamps also formed two arcs, symmetrical haloes',[19] that 'vaporeux' so redolent of the gaseous lack of fixity of modern life. (However, it should be pointed out that the French 'halo', used here, refers to physical phenomena, while it is 'auréole', the word used by Baudelaire, which also means a saintly or religious halo. The use here of 'halo' rather connotes the auratic, as we shall see.) The sexual interplay with figures emerging from the crowd in 'À une passante' (in fact, the poem's term, *éclair* or 'lightning flash' is used in *Lui*'s descriptions of gay cruising),[20] is replayed with greater force for the cruising homosexual because of his marginalised and minoritised position on the boulevards, but also in those areas his subculture has colonised, the *raison d'être* of which is for strangers in the night to exchange glances, for couplings to form and unform.

Moi marvels at the way the men having sex in the Tuileries emerge from the centre of the action, like dragonfly larvae mutating from 'vegetable agglomeration' to 'distinguished *flânerie*'.[21] Benjamin remarks of the *flâneur* – that leisured and invariably male wanderer of the city, poised for new experiences and the unearthing of new treasures – that he is to be distinguished from the man of the crowd, but is already in the mid-century an endangered species:

> Arcades where the *flâneur* would not be exposed to the sight of carriages that did not recognise pedestrians as rivals were enjoying undiminished popularity. There was the pedestrian who would let himself be jostled by the crowd, but there was also the *flâneur* who demanded elbow-room and was unwilling to forgo the life of a gentleman of leisure. Let the many attend to their daily affairs; the man of leisure can indulge in the perambulations of the *flâneur* only if as such he is already out of place.[22]

The *flâneur* is becoming an anachronism, partly because the fragility of his historical and social position means that he has to be in a situation where material urgencies are bracketed (*Moi* says of *Lui* that he could not imagine him working),[23] but where he is still engaged in the turmoil of the city. The urban homosexual fitted this description, feverishly sexually alert, nocturnally distant from his daytime labour of whatever class. To take that other dimension of modernity traced by Benjamin, the reconstruction of the inner self, its labour, perception and pleasures, through the stimuli of shock (be it the mechanics of factory work, the jostling and swerving of the street, or even the dodgem cars at a funfair),[24] it is interesting to note that in *Oiseau de la nuit* this is echoed in the ghost train in the Tuileries occupied by male couples,[25] or in the aleatory nature of cruising, and its temporal analogies with gambling and thus alienated factory work.[26]

The two further key elements in Benjamin's dissection of the contradictions of modernity are the aura and allegory. The aura is the uniqueness and authenticity of the object and the history or tradition it transmits. Perception of the aura is akin to the expectation we have when looking at people that they will return our gaze: 'To perceive the aura of an object we look at means to invest it with the ability to look at us in return.'[27] Modernity – and with it the mechanical reproduction of the work of art – witnesses the decline of the aura, and this is exemplified in Baudelaire in those poems in which there is an image of eyes which do not return the look, self-protective eyes, eyes characteristic of people on public transport, eyes of the prostitute looking for clients but also on guard against the police, 'the self-protective wariness of a wild animal hunting for prey'.[28] Whereas the symbol is fundamentally an idealising trope or mode of perception, introducing an element of spirit in a material object and thus posing as totalising harmony of 'being and signification',[29] the allegorical signifier, exemplified in Benjamin's early exploration of the seventeenth-century *Trauerspeil* or baroque drama, is mobile, arbitrary, on the surface of things, never at rest, located in a network of magical correspondences. There are adumbrations of these tropes in *Oiseau de la nuit*, the dramatisation of the decline of the aura in the exchange of glances in the gay café, the allegorical and not metaphorical aspects of the linguistic codes of the subculture, as we have seen. Benjamin's project, then, is to wrench these magic images from the tragic bad side of history, and to deploy them as the basis for alternative traditions and the new potentialities of the body.

The urban homosexual experience, then, can be read in Hocquenghem as an intensification of the aesthetic crises and transformations of modernity, in Benjamin's terms 'the manner in which human sense perception is organised, the medium in which it is accomplished',[30] and the historical circumstances in which this takes place. Promisingly, the daring dialectics of Benjamin permit a revolutionary or at least dissident aesthetics in the midst of commodity culture, as we shall see.

The late 1970s see the emergence of two other preoccupations which can be identified with a developing reflection on modernity. For Fourier, the society ushered in by the events of the 1790s in France was a travesty, not least because its greatest error had arguably been to reassert and not to abolish marriage and the family. The opportunity was lost of liberating women and children. For Hocquenghem and René Schérer in their collaborative work of 1976, *Co-ire: album systématique de l'enfance/Co-ire: systematic album of childhood*, childhood in this modern sense is about maintaining children in a state of non-productive torpor and – risky territory this – consent, deprived of autonomous means of existence, segregated in the institution of the family which is produced by the ideology of the couple. Hocquenghem and Schérer's text is on the one hand very Foucauldian. The segregation of children, the concomitant horror at children's vagabond status as well as the dread/desire expressed in much nineteenth-century literature of children snatched from their families, are all alibis for the Great Confinement, that event at the dawn of bourgeois society described by Foucault in *Histoire de la folie à l'âge classique* which removed the Other from any disruptive public role. The child is caught in panoptic fields (the metaphor from Foucault's *Surveiller et punir* for that internalising social surveillance characteristic of the prison cell observable from a central tower) which mean that he or she is always localised and observed in the institutions of school and family. (Hocquenghem and Schérer's 1974 article in *Les Temps modernes* emphasises the importance, in this process, of surveillance to prevent masturbation.)[31] The 'child' in modernity is thus characterised by the texture of a network of a 'play of forces' rather than 'psychological characteristics, inherent to a nature in itself'.[32] On the other hand, that very concept of nature is invoked to rebuff the admonition of an 1855 education manual that a child's obligation is to honour and respect the father, for Hocquenghem and Schérer the implantation of a 'truth so contrary to nature'.[33] Such hyperbolic flourishes are legitimised by the anti-personalism, anti-anthropomorphism and anti-*bildung* outlook that underpins their theory. As in Foucault, the subject or the person is the product of discipline, an example of the 'positive' as opposed to 'repressive' workings of power. In *Co-ire*, this notion is linked to what amounts in part to an adaptation of *Le Désir homosexuel* for children.

Invoking Deleuze's *Différence et répétition* of 1968, Hocquenghem and Schérer emphasise the fact that in the philosophical sense 'the person connotes not "the full positive enjoyment of the individual as such", that is, its "multiple, mobile, communicating" character, but a jealous withdrawal into the self, a distinction in principle between the bodily and the spiritual, an atomisation of private and incommunicable spheres'.[34] The child is disciplined into personhood. So what a liberation of the child actually means is the undermining of the adult/child distinction and the consequences of that for the liberation of all: 'childhood is not a fixed state which adulthood simply succeeds, but … there is a permanence of childhood that also concerns society in general'.[35] The place occupied by the child is in fact that of the immobilisation of fantasmatic wealth implied in the breakdown of the reality/fantasy distinction. An instrumental society nourished by the death of the child in everyone can be countered by a reinvestment in what the 'child' represents: 'The function of the child is to establish links, beauty, adornment, to break egoisms, to bring enthusiasm where people [*les personnes*] are content to talk about exchange.'[36] In particular, the child has a different relationship to its body as source of libidinal pleasure but also as something not delimited, as beyond the purely personal and anthropomorphic. Of course psychoanalysis strives to appropriate that polymorphousness through the process of Oedipalisation, as we saw in the previous chapter. The arguments of *Le Désir homosexuel* on desire and non-identity are here transposed (with Hocquenghem and Schérer in several provocative pages seeking even to discredit any causality in procreation). Childhood is thus a 'perverse function relative to the system which confines it, a function of the liberation, not of childhood as a distinct category, but of shackled energies'.[37] Children's bodies

are not yet organisms, they are like Deleuze and Guattari's Body
without Organs, surfaces of shifting intensities and potentialities,
incomplete in the sense of being unassigned to personhood and even
gender. They are complete in another sense, however, fully
erogenous, as opposed to the supremely ideological sexuality of
adults, centred on genitalia, often the phallus.

The argument, shifting from the aesthetic to the sexual, is also
concerned to legitimise sexual relations not only between children,
but, in certain forms, between children and adults. The implications of the essay's title, *Co-ire*, are of the promenade, going
together, a relationship with children outside school and family,
including (a certain form of) coitus. While this is not the place to
rehearse all the arguments around paedophilia,[38] it is noteworthy
that Hocquenghem and Schérer place such sexual activity in the
context of a transformed status of children, and seek to dislodge
genital-centred sex from its privileged position. And it is also true
that most adult–child sexual activity which occurs is in the family.
The argument that children's lot in contemporary society, with its
consequences for adult life, is one of the catastrophes of modernity,
is a strong one. However, the risks of such encounters are under-
estimated, as Hocquenghem and Schérer's discourse about consent
is decidedly woolly. It is one thing to argue that children should
be allowed to consent, and the fact that they are not is part of their
social disempowerment. (This is in fact Schérer's argument elsewhere
and the gist of a radio discussion in 1978 between Hocquenghem,
Foucault and Jean Danet, although here Hocquenghem insists
that a contractual notion of sexual consent is a nonsense.)[39] But
it is another, in the name of the joys of the molecular and non-anthropomorphic, to declare that 'the love between child and adult does
without dialogue and responsible, consenting persons'.[40] It is at
this point that the weakness of the link in Hocquenghem's theories
between an aesthetics and an ethics, let alone a praxis, is most
evident.

La Beauté du métis: réflexions d'un francophobe, published in 1979,
addresses that other phenomenon of modernity to emerge from the
French Revolution, namely the nation. However, rather than a
general analysis of the relationship between the European bourgeois
revolution and nation-making, the deliberate hyperbole of
Hocquenghem's scathing and often hilarious diatribe targets the
prime originator, the French nation, 'le système France' which
represents itself as a master model, but which for him is the quin-
tessence of the worst that the idea of the nation embodies: 'it is
not the world which is made up of homoethic and incommunicable
nationalities, just a certain vision of the world produced by French
history',[41] 'the most successful model for preventing audacities of
spirit and adventures of the body'.[42] The familiar vocabulary of

nomadism, flows and drives is harnessed at this collective political level: '*Métis* [mixed race, hybrid], emigrant, combining within yourself the inexhaustible forces of multiple identities, you disperse being-there into contradictory signs.'[43] Needless to say, the *étranger* (foreigner, stranger, outsider) is important not for any full identity he or she may promise or claim, but for the knock-on effect of the destabilisation of identities, 'to be "with" what is elsewhere, not to be oneself elsewhere but someone else somewhere else'.[44]

Faced with the world's 'festive cosmopolitan tumult', France (or 'france' as Hocquenghem writes it) and the French are 'immobile'.[45] The bulk of *La Beauté du métis* is devoted not to beauty but to ugliness, to France. The immigrant is to be assimilated or expelled, the foreigner is a visitor or an enemy. A state centralised early has none of the incoherences of Germany and Italy. A country without a history of emigration could never produce those transoceanic communities of the British, Spanish (and Portuguese) empires, or offspring which would come to surpass and dominate their home culture. The reluctance to co-mingle with the Other explains the French anti-hero(ine) par excellence, the adulterous woman (witness the Liberation period). Indeed French misogyny and homophobia are understood as fear that they are as one with *l'étranger*[46] (although, in a reverse movement, there are therefore problems with Hocquenghem's description of France as an 'old maid'). Above all, it is *le fonctionnariat*, that welding of the state and its bureaucracy, with its classifications, rigidities and centralisation in Paris, that are responsible for the closure and immobility. Whereas the modern nation-state is now universal, in other countries the state is at best impatiently tolerated and perceived as domination, whereas in France it is the summum of civilisation and culture, solicited and sought after. The events of 1789 were simply the reinforcement of centralised state structures created by absolutism, and of the classical aesthetic of geometry and coherence. The history of the Republic is about order; revolutions, including May 1968, represent a return to order after a brief period of chaos, unlike those of other countries (England, the USA, even Russia?) which have represented some evolution or movement forward. No significant cultural movement takes place from the periphery to the centre, everything is centre to periphery, top-down. Regional and popular culture is disdained. Language is bureaucratised in the *Académie française*, its first members admonished to 'cleanse the language of the filth contracted in the mouths of the people or in the palace crowd'.[47] French childhoods are excruciating, a child in this system is 'an inhibited little bureaucrat, an accountant for its emotions'.[48] Paris is a Foucauldian 'eye of surveillance'.[49]

Making allowances for this text's exaggeration and provocation, there is much that rings true for any *étranger* who has resided in

France. What is more, on the eve of the 1980s and the resurgence of the *Front national*, Hocquenghem is prescient in pinpointing these limitations of French culture, and is fired to cast his theoretical eye on the subject long before other French intellectuals, such as Julia Kristeva (whose *Etranger à nous-mêmes*, for example, was published ten years later). His dismissal of the sterility of French music would happily be surpassed by the very *métissé* 'world music' phenomenon centred on Paris in the 1980s. While François Mitterrand would invoke the republican humanist tradition to counter the *Front national*, sow disarray in the right-wing opposition and win the presidential election of 1988, Hocquenghem would no doubt see this as insufficient and a temporary, opportunistic manoeuvre (if we recall the *Lettre ouverte*). More importantly, the invective of *La Beauté du métis* involves Hocquenghem in writing out of his analysis the *métissage* which has existed in French culture, be it Yves Montand or Isabelle Adjani, as well as confirming through his (master) discourse the invalidation of regional or popular struggle and cultural forms. The anathematisation of the state in favour of a 'free trade' in cultures, flows and bodies, has of course its admirable side but fails, on the eve of the liberal economic orthodoxies of the 1980s, to acknowledge any paradox or problem. Like many of the Parisian intellectuals he condemns, Hocquenghem suffers from a PCF complex, which blocks his view of the left, of the state, and of the working class. His diatribe is very France-centred, a point he nearly acknowledges when he argues that much recent French philosophy (Foucault, Deleuze, Glucksmann) can be analysed as a response to the specificities of the French state. His vocabulary of drives and flows confirms the view that the solution to 'le système France' is not an Anglo-Saxon civil society to mediate between state and individual, and this is crucial to his view of 'sexual minorities'. For our immediate purposes in this chapter, the question arises of periodisation: when does *métissage*, with accompanying phenomena such as emigration, become impossible? Has it always existed? Is it a factor of modernity which France loses out on because of its peculiar history, or one of post-modernity which sclerotic French structures contradict?

Recapitulating Hocquenghem's views so far on modernity, we can say that the Enlightenment era ushered in a social and economic order based on instrumental rationalism, capitalism, nationalism, the family, and technology. In Foucauldian terms, the heterogeneity of 'life' was replaced by the homogenising construction of subjects with a conscience. However, just as this process of the construction of the 'homosexual' identity, replacing the scattered, non-totalised acts of 'sodomy', was two-way, productive as well as delimiting, so did the lifestyles and spaces of modernity yield raw material for resistance and dissent. In the modern city, homosexuality and delinquency, the *parcours* of a marginalised subculture, intensified the paradoxical poetic resonances of the new urban landscape. In addition, the Nietzschean emphasis on perpetual becoming, taken up of course in *L'Anti-Oedipe*, exults in the possibilities that modernity has created, the journeys of experience, energy and position made possible by its destabilising maelstrom.[50] Hocquenghem can thus be seen to maintain contact with both the positive and negative sides of modernity.

However, as we saw in his *Lettre ouverte* of 1986, what he tentatively and rather unhelpfully terms the contemporary 'post-modern' age has abandoned the inventive dialectic of possibilities of the modern. French society of the 1980s is given over to the 'real', the instrumental, *raison d'état*, nationalism, conformism and consumerism. The decline of Marxist ideologies has accompanied a more generalised loss of critical dissent. This is all the more worrying as that society has emerged from the apparently dissident modernist politics of May 1968 and the social movements that followed. May 1968 proved to be both the end of one era – the revolutionary but also aesthetic *mise en scène* of barricades in the Paris streets – and the ushering in of another, the 'modernisation' of French capitalist society, as we have seen. The FHAR was superseded by a mainstreaming re-regulation of same-sex desire which for Hocquenghem is totally unsatisfactory. Hedonism, available to only a tiny minority of anti-bourgeois artists earlier in the century, has via the demands for pleasure of May 1968 become a generalised accommodation within the economic system. Moreover, in the vocabulary of *L'Anti-Oedipe* for example, it can be a fine line in advanced consumer society between what relentlessly deterritorialising capitalism enables the body to do, and what it limits: 'The actualisation of the capitalist state transforms a body's degrees of freedom into a bifurcating network, not of virtual futures for the body to become, but of possible objects a consumer might own.'[51] Nevertheless, contemporary society has expanded the body's realms of possibility, demolarising humanity in the fields of image production and consumption.

One can see how deeply worrying this would be for Hocquenghem, so concerned to preserve dissent and a freedom of becoming, while at the same time perturbed to see the fruits of his generation's activity producing a caricature of civilised life. His disenchantment with the orthodoxies of contemporary life is radical, and he is not prone to home in on the possibilities for a radicalising of democracy in the personal and social spheres glimpsed by Anthony Giddens in the links between modernity's accelerating abandonment of the frameworks of tradition, the increase in personal autonomy, and the emergence of a plastic sexuality freed from the intrinsic link with reproduction.[52] The question remains, however, from what

position can Hocquenghem question contemporary society and offer
ways forward? We have seen that the view of the late Frankfurt
School, partly articulated in Mario Mieli's text, relies too heavily
on notions of an authentic critical consciousness which is repressed
and distorted by consumerism, source of a negative aesthetics
which awaits its emergence in a communist future. As a consequence,
this view faces contemporary life rather undialectically (for example,
Mieli writes, 'the stinking metropolis is the negation of sight'),[53]
as it relies on a monolithic, non-contradictory concept of ideology
holding the social order in place. Its emphasis is on the totality of
conditions, and not local particularities. As far as theories of 'post-
modernism' are concerned, while their emphasis on the undermining
of binary oppositions structured by hierarchy and power, for
example between high and low culture, or in discourses of race and
gender, may productively set free all sorts of local pluralities and
pleasures, they often lack a critical negativity and fall into complicity
with the given fluidities of consumer capitalism, the danger that
haunts Hocquenghem in the 1980s. In addition, of course, they
may fail to perceive the coexistence of 'modern' and 'post-modern'
cultural forms in a society or even an individual's habitus, since
the proclamation of the 'post-modern' may paradoxically participate in a master narrative of 'before' and 'after'.

The construction of a critical negativity is of course dependent
on a positivity, and while Hocquenghem might eschew the Hegelian
certainties of consciousness embedded in Frankfurt School theory,
his earlier emphasis on desire and the molecular may come to his
aid. Co-written with René Schérer, L'Ame atomique ('The Atomic
Soul' a pun on 'arme' or 'weapon'), published in 1986, is the philosophical counterpart of that year's Lettre ouverte. As we shall see,
it daringly overturns a 'bad side' of capitalist modernity, namely
the atomisation of social life that is often critiqued,[54] and wittily
offers a riposte to the totalising nuclear orthodoxies of the French
national state. Its subtitle is 'for an aesthetics of the nuclear age',
and it is worth reflecting on what is at stake in the term. In what
way is 'aesthetics' central to the problems of (post)modernity?

As Terry Eagleton argues, the philosophical preoccupation with
the aesthetic since the Enlightenment is 'inseparable from the construction of the dominant ideological forms of modern class society,
and indeed from a whole new form of human subjectivity appropriate to that social order'.[55] Contradictorily, it combines notions
of sensuous particularity (its etymology connects with the verb 'to
feel') with abstract formulation. With the advent of capitalist society
and the reign of the commodity, the work of art or artefact becomes
separate and autonomous, mirroring the bourgeois ideological
myth that we as human subjects exist for ourselves and owe nothing
to anyone, but also positing a realm of freedom in which human

powers may surpass market utility. The now free-floating category of the aesthetic is a way of replacing the coercion of absolutism, of marrying the general and the particular, and of balancing individual antagonism and indeed atomisation in the social and economic spheres with the inner binding coherence of the subject's appetites, inclinations and affections.[56] This process is one of both oppression and of utopianism. Its history since 1750 offers various mutations. In the late nineteenth century and the increasing reification of capitalist society, the aesthetic of modernism, announced in Baudelaire and articulated by Benjamin for example, emphasises the autonomy of art, its role as negation, as 'the guerrilla tactics of secret subversion, of silent resistance, of stubborn refusal'.[57] Postwar consumer capitalism, however, sees a wholesale aestheticisation of society as culture becomes increasingly commodified.

The diagnosis of contemporary society to be found in *L'Ame atomique* has its roots in the critique of the instrumental rationalism of modernity, and its political and institutional failures. Concurring with Adorno that the post-Auschwitz reality calls into question that totalising Enlightenment legacy which strives to render the identity of concept or thought with the thing or the world, the project of Hocquenghem and Schérer's volume is to 'explore other avenues', as 'political reason has now only to keep silent'.[58] In the catastrophe of modernity, the closure of myths – as limiting as those scrutinised by Barthes in *Mythologies* – confines 'individuals without individuality',[59] whose lives are in fact 'in bits', in 'a system which works by itself'.[60] Mass culture is not in fact totally rejected – Hocquenghem and Schérer approvingly quote Baudrillard's *A l'ombre des majorités silencieuses* to praise the 'brilliant apathy' of the masses which undoes or negates the totalisation of ideology, and we shall see that some audio-visual technology is co-opted to their aesthetics – but its dominant practices certainly are:

> Today, the levelling down caused by the democracy of the vulgar [*trivial*] is called mass culture or media information: it is expressed in opinion polls, the quest for individual, ethnic or racial identities, in which banalised 'difference' becomes a homage to the norm.[61]

What is 'bad' in contemporary society, then, is the prosaic, flatness, realism, the concept, determinism, myth, ideology, but also 'personalism': 'A permanent return to personalism is complementary and not antagonistic to the dictatorship of technical imperatives.'[62] Since the 'self' and the 'human' are the creations of modernity and thus supremely ideological, Hocquenghem and Schérer move to short-circuit this process. It is at this point that they move away from the dialectical thought so crucial to Adorno, who recognises the need for fragile, provisional notions of identity, with its claims to be total, if the non-identity of the particulars of the world is to be dissonant and negating. Their strategy is to prioritise 'the world' and our place in it, rather than seek to salvage Enlightenment's original promise of freely interrelating, autonomous individual consciousnesses.

The oxymoronic 'atomic soul' is most certainly not metaphysical: 'The soul reduced to its metaphysical, humanist form is, like the body confined within its organic form, a reactive abstraction, a limit to overcome.'[63] Hocquenghem and Schérer juxtapose the idea of the soul lost with the advent of modernity – with its connotations of the infinite, the opening out to the universe, the irreducible non-closure of the poetic – with the atom, the fragment, the particle, the bits of which everything is made and by which everything happens, a source of unity. The atom is both material and unrepresentable. The inspiration, boldly, comes from both antiquity and contemporary science. The didactic poem *De Rerum Natura* (*On the Nature of the Universe*) by Lucretius debunks the myths of gods prevailing over our destinies, of a finished cosmos, by invoking a metaphysics of the particle. The universe has no centre. It consists of atoms that move, collide, enter into combinations. They transmit sensory signals, they assemble and disperse. (As Hocquenghem and Schérer point out, this is also true of language, its arrangements and reshuffling of 'letters', the Latin *elementa*.)[64] The universe is thus a question of creative, dynamic play, and is therefore indeterminate, open rather than closed, as the swerving movement of the atoms in the void – without which their fall would be simply vertical and formless – is unpredictable. This philosophy was the basis of Epicureanism, built not on instrumentalism and action but on pleasure, not in a narrow hedonistic sense but in the inclusive sense of well-being, the sensual and the serene. Handily, developments in contemporary physics such as catastrophe theory, randomness as opposed to causal determinism, as well as the shifting and vibrating sub-atomic particles of quantum theory, form the scientific 'grounding' for the discourse of *L'Ame atomique*, even as the work seeks to extend such observations into the realms of art and society. Technology as such, therefore, is not the radical antonym of this philosophical and aesthetic project. Subtly, while Hocquenghem and Schérer reject 'the mythologised nonsense of a technoculture',[65] they see the latter as part of a uniformising *process* that depends on the link between personalism and automatism. Thus a computer game may have its place in their aesthetic, for the visionary nature of the 'abrupt fulgurations' on its screen that 'concretise the injunctions of the soul' are to be preferred to 'the information-driven, realist and programmed television screen'.[66]

Such manoeuvres are possible because of the emphasis on the overcoming of the boundaries between the self and universe, and the aesthetic priority given to those intermittences between man and machine, nature and artifice, real and illusion. We here seem to be back in the territory of *L'Anti-Oedipe*: 'the soul ... is not the transition towards the apprenticeship of personal identity',[67] but a Body without Organs. However, this potentiality cannot be limited to desire alone: 'Those who limit themselves by speaking the language of desire still remain on the threshold of the soul, which is unlimited.'[68] Connections are always there, for the 'subject' inhabits and is inhabited by a continuum of space, time and substance: 'an animated, active, erotic, aesthetic, passionate spatiality' which 'also includes time, the memory-image'.[69] Making use of the airy connotations of the wide-open circumflexed vowel in the French *âme;* Hocquenghem and Schérer thus emphasise processes of dilation, expansion, dispersion, dressing the Kantian idea of the incommensurate with the scientific and science fiction vocabulary of the aesthetic as the 'things from another world'.[70] Meanwhile, they insist on the critical value of the aesthetic in terms of, especially, Fourier and Baudelaire (via Benjamin) rather than Adorno:

> when Baudelaire himself invents and names the aesthetic category of 'modernity', it is in order to bring into the field of the artist everything which seemed excluded from it, to enrich art with what around him is becoming, as much as to reveal, after the ultra-modern Fourier, the backwards march and the deception of progress.[71]

Rather than reproduce the architecture of *L'Ame atomique* which structures the argument around four 'aesthetic categories' (Souls, Visions, Allegories and the Sublime) interrupted by playful and speculative interludes, my procedure here is to follow at a sometimes more atomic level a number of concepts that can be tracked through the work's argument, and then to re-alight on the contrasting aesthetic landmarks in modernity that are Fourier and Kant. The first is that of *constellation*. Invoked for example to describe the heterogeneous aesthetic categories examined by Hocquenghem and Schérer,[72] it derives from Rilke and Benjamin and is important for its rejection of teleological history based on linear causality. Objects are to be understood not via a governing central idea, but via a disarticulation into disparate elements viewed from a myriad of angles, a procedure which thus permits the cultivation of discontinuities in the forward march of modernity and rational progress. The process of *diffraction*, as for example in the surprises of the modern city, is that of the deviation of light, of the detail that suggests passions and particularities, of beauty in the midst of degradation. In the domain of historical transformation, the notion of progress is diffracted by that of catastrophe and vice versa, and thus the pos-

sibility of the new and even salvation, a Messianic view of what can
be blasted out of history that again owes much to Benjamin:

> The historical theory of catastrophe, between origin and destruc-
> tion, ruin and affirmation, snatches from the past its unfulfilled
> promises. If, looking closer, the continuity of progress is but the
> mythical diffraction of a succession of catastrophes, then history,
> at any moment, can take another course, a turn of salvation.[73]

Détournement is a strategic version of this, whether in a child's
questioning of instrumentality, or in the *parcours* and gaze of the
man in the crowd or *flâneur* (as in Baudelaire, equated by
Hocquenghem and Schérer): 'cruising and *flânerie* take hold of the
very things which, in the urban decor, ought to incite to work, science
and patriotism'.[74] *Détournement* is of course also a situationist
concept, as when for example Vaneigem argues for a turning round,
a reclamation of lost meaning that puts the stasis of the spectacle
in motion.[75] However, Hocquenghem and Schérer argue that the
notion of the *aura* contradicts the situationist notion (as in Guy
Debord's *Society of the Spectacle*) that we are in alienation, in thrall
to the spectacular, to the falsity of contemporary images. The
Benjaminian aura can be found anywhere, it appears and disappears
in its fragmentary, chaotic, allegorical and inexplicable way, a new
magic or phantasmagoria rather than a source of nostalgia or
political protest. It indicates

> the other aspect of this society of shocks, of uniformisation, of
> masses. Each person [or thing] hides the most romantic
> [*romanesque*, romantic, novel-like] of intimacies, has a double
> face for those who can glimpse it, but only in a flash, in that
> instant of illumination in which the shadow of a doubt strikes
> us about the shadow we have just passed.[76]

In terms familiar from *Co-ire*, the *child* is the incomplete and even
non-anthropomorphic, a privileged vehicle for the passions and play
of the atomic soul. The child's relationship with machines and dolls,
its naivety and undermining of the serious, all point to an inter-
mediary zone between subject and object. Notably, we are all
child-like when faced with colours (evacuated by and large from
modern male dress). Colour is both abstract and sensual, the possibility of escape, beyond messages and signification, its perception
as source of light is a clue to the juxtapositions of elements that
make up the world. The notion of *correspondances* – as in Baudelaire's
famous poem of the same name, in which different sense impres-
sions, smell and touch, for example, refer to each other, a process
known as synaesthesia – is relevant for Kandinsky's attitude to colour
but also to *allegory* in the Benjaminian sense. Whereas the received
notion of allegory, of one-to-one equivalences and of the personi-

fication of abstract categories, is discredited in the Romantic and post-Romantic tradition of Goethe, Hegel and Lukács,[77] Hocquenghem and Schérer turn the negative of its anti-individualism into a positive, linking it to their anti-anthropomorphism and even to the aesthetic promise held out by the overcoming of the binary between living and non-living matter. Moreover, they locate allegory, and the putting-into-allegory (*allégorèse* or allegoresis, as 'seme' – 'meaning' is to 'semiosis', the production of meaning) in precisely those historical moments when belief in direct communication with a truth or god (the domain of the, for them, anathematised 'myth') has broken down: 'Its internal tension is that of an irreducible contradiction between the loss of the sacred as stable signification, and a universal charge of undefined signification, fluttering above everything.'[78] The overcoming of the distinction between reality and fantasy, the element of mystery and enigma, which is ultimately linked to the play of attraction linking the desiring body and the particles of the atomic soul, can be detected in the dissident allegorising of the cruising homosexual in the modern city, but also as a discontinuous, alternative tradition in the master narrative of the West, in those negative theologies and syncretisms such as the first-century Gnostic Christian heresy, with its notion of an unknowable and hidden God beyond the devalued world created by that vindictive demiurge, the Jehovah of the Old Testament.

The centrality of the *baroque* in the aesthetic of *L'Ame atomique* is thus due to its endlessly proliferating meaning, its contradiction of classical order and measure, its cosmopolitanism and its syncretic mingling of figures from Christianity and paganism at a time when the unity of belief and meaning was under threat. The dispersed, dynamic and multipolar world of the baroque is an aesthetic of becoming, it lays bare the vitality which underpins both history and nature: nature is made strange and monstrous, history loses its security of belief. This aesthetic is crucial to the possibilities of vision that modernity in fact contains behind and beyond its objectivising and perspectivising gaze. Hocquenghem and Schérer's critique of modern vision can usefully be compared with that of 1970s' and 1980s' *Screen* theory in Britain. Stephen Heath, for example, argues that the *quattrocento* perspective, implying a single point of view and the isomorphism of space, coincided with the construction of a new form of subjectivity, one which we would recognise as bourgeois and which is the ancestor of the procedures of classical Hollywood cinema.[79] Hocquenghem and Schérer argue that the modern gaze has its secret, alternative visionary tradition, for that 'single point of view' is in fact multiple, given the number of 'points of view' which now exist in the world, but it is also a relation of attraction and passion. Sight is now a question of knowledge, but knowing depends on seeing. The 'will to know' is also 'the desire to see everything'.[80] The unified bourgeois subject is a myth constructed out of a world of atoms in which no space is empty, and within which living beings are simply the structurally stable singularities: 'Modernity was constituted in, and constructed, the continuum of space; it simultaneously dominated it and lost itself there. But we shall go further: space can threaten the living with this loss only because it is itself living.'[81] So, rather than a stable subject position being created out of a process of suture in relation to the moving image, Hocquenghem and Schérer prefer Deleuze's account of the cinema in which that process is dominated and replaced by a process of 'vaporisation of the real', of appearances and disappearances: 'The eye is in things.'[82]

The nearest *L'Ame atomique* gets to a theory of ethics is in the section on melancholy, seen as that excess, that impossible aspiration to the divine and the infinite faced with the rationalisations of the modern era. However, Hocquenghem and Schérer insist that this is an aesthetic, not a political category, one which calls into question that binary opposition in the context of our helplessness faced with a (now) inaccessible history. The concepts of the incommensurate and of the sublime are crucial to this discussion, and obviously lead us to an examination of the uses Hocquenghem and Schérer make of Kant.

The Kantian system relies on a duality. We move in two simultaneous but incompatible worlds, those of noumena and phenomena. The former are those things knowable to thought alone, and therefore unknowable, because it is only the latter, the world of appearances, of objects of possible experience, which is fortuitously accessible to, and corresponds with, our conceptual and intuitive or sense categories. Pure reason always aspires to know the unconditioned, to know the world outside and beyond individual perspective. Practical reason deals not with truths but with duty, in the moral law that reason provides through the categorical imperative, and in the exercise of freedom. It can thus be argued that the Kantian subject is split: we are both noumenal subjects of a transcendental freedom that grounds universal value, and phenomenal objects in nature that are determined facts (although the object-in-itself, beyond our categories, is always unknowable). The account of the aesthetic to be found in the *Critique of Judgement* of 1790 offers a mediation between pure and practical reason, noumen and phenomenon. Through the workings of imagination rather than theory, the aesthetic involves both a sensory experience and a claim to universality through the construction of a community of free, feeling subjects. In this abstraction of our interests and desires, the aesthetic object is perceived as an end in itself, purposiveness without purpose, but also in a striving beyond the limits of our point of view and a glimpsing of the possibility of a non-alienated object. The sublime, that glimpse of the infinite in the work of art or nature, interacts dialectically with the beautiful, that realisation of our correspondence to reality, a process that thus involves both comprehension and incomprehensibility, the sensory and the suprasensory, our fittedness to the world but also our limitations.

At the dawn of modernity, then (Kant was writing against absolutism in a not fully developed bourgeois society), we find delineated and theoretically encapsulated a 'solution' to the subject/object dilemma, one which validates both the sovereignty of the individual subject and the reality of the objective world. This is crucial to the political and property systems of modernity, but it is a precarious solution. It has its (liberal) utopian element in the celebration of freedom and the ideal of a community of rational subjects, but is riven with the contradictions of the emerging middle-class society. We are both free and unfree, sovereign subjects of liberty and objects governed by necessity in the anonymous play of economic forces. In a post-feudal world in which 'what to do?' cannot be deduced from your social position, ethics thus has to become self-referential, and the aesthetic is in turn modelled on this, reconciling pure thought with concrete sense experience, a global decree with material particularity.

For Hocquenghem and Schérer in *L'Ame atomique*, Kant is read and adjusted for his utopian potential, and then set up to be surpassed by another figure of his epoch. The Kantian dialectic of the sublime and the beautiful is about both propping up and humbling the subject, and for a Marxist critic like Eagleton this is part of its ideological effect, its naturalising of social norms as it brings us out of ourselves and puts us back, renewed and refreshed, into the world. However, Hocquenghem and Schérer alight upon that aspect of the sublime which is 'a kind of unconscious process of infinite desire, which like the Freudian unconscious continually risks swamping and overloading the pitiable ego with an excess of affects'.[83] While they approve his break from the notion that the rules of classical form are what constitutes the beautiful, as well as the 'negative theology' involved in the incommensurate and the unrepresentable, their own interpretation of the sublime emphasises its dynamic and transformative power: a 'movement' which ensures 'the transformation of an inert world into a universe of latent forces'.[84] Noting one of its etymologies in the distillations of medieval alchemy, they proclaim its sensuality: 'The sublime spiritualises, but only in so much as it elevates and concentrates the sensual to a higher power ... It transforms, it refines or purifies by going from ascension to concentration. It reinforces the erotic instead of renouncing it.'[85] Kant stops short of the baroque, with its refusal of conciliation in nature. Hocquenghem and Schérer con-

centrate on the subject-shattering or decentring aspect of the
sublime, that floating between being and nothingness which constitutes its threshold, and argue that Kant in the end domesticates
and tames it. What interests them is the way in which a resistance
to modernity, and in particular its hegemonic rational-scientific
domination of nature, is adumbrated in Kantian theory even as it
constitutes it.

The glimpses of utopianism in Kant's aesthetic are also there in
his 1795 essay, *Perpetual Peace*, written in the midst of European
war. Its argument is basically for a world federation of republican
nation-states trading with each other. It translates into the political
field some major aspects of Kant's philosophy, notably that
Enlightenment belief in humanity's progress toward rationality, and
the role of morality, reason and free will – a general, civic will – in
bringing such a world about. Thus Kant's peace requires 'the
uniformity of the human race and the universality of the moral
person'.[86]

Against Kant, Hocquenghem and Schérer play Fourier. Where
Kant's moral law is aesthetic in form, grounded in reason, and
describes a fissure between politics and culture, in Fourier form
and content are united in the organisation of passions; the *domestique*
(that space of passionate attractions) invades the political, the
personal and the anthropomorphic are surpassed. Fourier's hostility
to commerce and capitalism means that the 'subjects' of his utopia
('Harmony') do not need to police the boundaries of self and
other, nor resist their own inclinations in their exercise of (moral)
choice. The 'immorality' of the passions in Civilisation is due to
their repression or distortion, whereas in Harmony they construct
a universal morality based on the free and indeed baroque association of series of, not abstractions, but sensory pleasures.

In this way, a work like Fourier's *Théorie des quatre mouvements*
of 1808 is set up by Hocquenghem and Schérer as the antithesis
of Kant's *Perpetual Peace*. Fourier announces a wholesale resistance
to the modernity born out of the French Revolution. The idea of
progress is rejected in favour of a theory of historical catastrophe
(we can see the affinity with Benjamin), a term which denotes both
the historical events of the Terror and the development of capitalism,
but which also provides an opportunity to read the morphogene-
sis of historical change across discontinuous phases. Similarly,
Kant's liberal federation of nation-states is incompatible with his
own notion of cosmopolitan right. In contrast, Fourier favours the
(unfulfilled and unexplored) possibilities opened up by the monopoly
of empire (in his era, that of Bonaparte), more likely in any case
than capitalist nation-states to promote peace and a new passionate
social order: 'Uniteism [Fourier's notion of cosmopolitanism, of
adopting the tone of the other] establishes the free play of differ-

ences across the surface of the globe.'[87] Whereas Kant's dualism
of morality and politics has him construct the notion of the 'publicity
of maxims', the public guarantee of the workings of reason whereby
nation-states would openly declare the principles by which they are
operating, and would thus by definition never do anything immoral
or aggressive, Fourier's 'publicity of the passions', in which all desires
are avowed, would transform world society into associations devoted
to their enjoyment. Kant's erasure of politics in favour of morality
is countered by one of Fourier's quainter notions, the conserva-
tion of politics in exclusively formal terms, as those turned on by
intrigue and even war indulge themselves in pure spectacle for the
enjoyment of all.

The implications of the particular influence of the
Fourier specialist René Schérer in these final pages of *L'Ame
atomique*, it is pointless to speculate on the relative investment of
the two authors in phases of their argument, and in any case they
both put their names to the whole work. Clearly, they do not
believe Fourier's utopia can be put into practice now or hence.
Rather, they seek to posit a field, something beyond the negative
dialectics of, say, the Frankfurt School, which can represent the
end towards which a politics that differs from contemporary orthodoxies may aspire.[88] Although the obvious critique of bourgeois
capitalist society is to be found in Marx, Hocquenghem and Schérer
stress all that is non-totalising, non-anthropomorphic, aesthetic,
sexual-political and even sexy in Fourier's agenda, with the implication that he requires a dusting-off greater than the semiotic
analysis provided by Roland Barthes in 1971.[89] Although Marx is
kind to Fourier, he is much more positive than the latter about the
achievements of capitalism and the bourgeoisie, and is clearly
more sanguine about the family and the nation-state, seeking to
overcome bourgeois society dialectically rather than negate it cata-
strophically. Hocquenghem and Schérer also fail to address the
problem of Fourier's naturalism, the grounding of his passions and
their schemas in nature, and how this can be made compatible with
Hocquenghem's previous use of Foucault.

The implications of *L'Ame atomique* for the sexual agendas set
by Hocquenghem in the 1970s will be be discussed in the final
chapter. Suffice it to say at present that the utopian vision of the
'empire of seduction' is founded for Hocquenghem, as all decent
utopias should be, in the possibilities of the past and the present
rather than the future. The phenomenon of transcultural 'com-
munications between identical or different sensibilities',[90] including
the uniformisation in consumer culture of (deliberately unnamed
and unspecified) gay sex ('secret mores, interracial and international cruising or pick-ups')[91] is thus significant as a source of

possible diffraction of imperialism that mocks the boundaries of
the nation-state, and as grounded in passions and inclinations
rather than (full) identities. It forgets, perhaps, the necessary con-
stitution, for this transforming vision, of, for example, that
international gay tourism so satirised in the 1970s.

The consumerist limitations of contemporary culture are what
Jean-François Lyotard denounces as mere 'eclecticism'[92] as opposed
to his definition of the post-modern as that aesthetic which in its
content and its form shatters in the modern the nostalgia for the
unattainable 'whole and the one, for the reconciliation of the
concept and the sensible, of the transparent and the communicable
experience'.[93] Hocquenghem and Schérer owe much of their
attempt at defining the post-modern to Lyotard, who notably
draws a curtain over the master narratives of the West such as the
Enlightenment belief in progress and *bildung*, and Marxism.
However, their use of the term 'post-modern' is extremely unsys-
tematic. We are far from the totalising Lukácsian categories of Fredric
Jameson, who argues that in contemporary culture the 'modern',
with its concepts of alienation, authenticity and interpretation, has
definitely given way to the 'post-modern', with its play of surfaces,
emphasis on signifier rather than signified, and cult of the present.
We are not even in the realm of Lyotard, with his local resistances
and language games. They may concur with one critic who argues
that modernity was characterised by myth (negatively charged in
L'Ame atomique) and post-modernity by ritual, but thereby confer
on the residues of myth, the rituals without belief of contemporary life, a source of resistance because of the absence they invoke.[94]
What they generally mean by the 'post-modern' is that combination of ideas that proclaims the 'end of ideology' in the decline of
the myths of modernity (itself an ideology, as they point out),
while simultaneously embracing technology and capitalism and
closing off possibilities for historical and cultural change: that
immobility and contraction within Parisian intellectual orthodoxy
attacked in the *Lettre ouverte*, coupled with the retreat into 'full' but
restrictive national and cultural identities.

Hocquenghem and Schérer are seeking to surpass both those
totalising myths of modernity and the conservatism disavowed or
otherwise in the contemporary world. In fact, they are nearer to
Anthony Giddens's argument that the 'post-modern' is yet to
come, and that we are living in an intensification and to a certain
extent radicalisation of those aspects of modernity born two hundred
years ago. The '"post-modern" condition' is also 'extremely
modern',[95] the philosophical traditions Hocquenghem and Schérer
trace lead us 'to that other, within us, which dreams of overcoming
the modern, and even the sleeping sphinx of post-modernity'.[96] At
one point they declare themselves to be '*épimodernes*', [97] from the

Greek preposition 'on', as in epidermis, epicentre, or more usefully epicycle, that astronomical image of circles within circles.

If it is indeed true that for several years until his death, the questioning of modernity was Hocquenghem's 'constant pre-occupation',[98] then *Oiseau de la nuit, Co-ire, La Beauté du métis* and *L'Ame atomique* bear witness to the richness of that reflection. Hocquenghem succeeds in salvaging something from the wreckage of modernity, and ceaselessly upholds the possibilities and openness that a non-linear and non-teleological history hold out. However, two questions arise: what kind of politics or praxis, what kind of art for this cultural and historical moment? Or is this perhaps one question, given the priority given to the aesthetic? Answers partly lie in a telling description *Moi* makes of *Lui* in *Oiseau de la nuit*: 'He was the spontaneous philosopher of the only credible absolutes in today's world, he used his *consubstantial particularity* to hollow himself into a concave mirror concentrating the revealing opposite pole of our advanced societies.'[99] This can be understood as a cult of the particular which has broken free from the link with the universal characteristic of post-Kantian aesthetics, and has therefore no role to play in the construction of social hegemonies; or it is a variation on the notion of the particular in the form of either the typical (realism) or the exceptional (modernism) embodying a certain knowledge ('revealing') of contemporary society; or it is an attempt to get beyond these dichotomies, as in *L'Ame atomique* when a universal is conjured out of particles, particulars and passions. Hocquenghem's five novels ring the changes on these approaches to art.

4

Fictions

This section concentrates on four of Hocquenghem's five novels: *L'Amour en relief/Love in relief* (1982, the only one so far to be translated into English), *La Colère de l'agneau/The Wrath of the Lamb* (1985), *Eve* (1987), and *Les Voyages et aventures extraordinaires du frère Angelo/The Extraordinary Voyages and Adventures of Brother Angelo* (1988). The novelistic output dominates his activities in the 1980s, and thus the years prior to his death in August 1988, for several reasons. His primary journalistic occupation was coming to an end in 1981–82, in the disputes with Serge July at *Libération*, as we have seen. It was prolonged only briefly in work at the radio station Europe 1. In addition, his public roles, as 'homosexual militant' and as post-*soixante-huitard* media figure, had become philosophically distasteful and politically problematic, given the assumption of power by members of his generation, and the relative mainstreaming of a certain middle-class gay culture, processes accelerated by the electoral victories of the Socialists in 1981. The turn to history and the aesthetic discussed in the previous chapter marked a preoccupation with the long term, whether in the discourses around 'homosexuality' or indeed the whole of modern life.

Oiseau de la nuit was not his first work of fiction. A collection of short stories, *Fin de section/End of Section*, published in 1975, prolongs some of the reflections on May 1968 to be found in *L'Après-mai des faunes* of the previous year. Formal experimentation (a 'schizophrenic' child in *Maintenant c'est différent/Now It's Different*, a collage of cassette transcripts in *Croix du sud/Southern Cross*, a projection in the future – 1979 – narrated from yet further in the future in *Faux printemps/False Spring*) coexists with a preoccupation with the fate of the 1968 generation in its public and private life, and with the desire to push back, nomad-like, the frontiers of 'the real'. The dilemma is summed up by the narrator of the title story:

> I was at that time ... obsessed by the fear of missing the great work. The decline of revolutionary metaphysics, which had until then given me the necessary tension, washed me up with many others on that notorious beach haunted by publishers and young talents.[1]

The apparent binary oppositions in this sentence, from sublime meaning and direction to the absurdities of the social comedy, are in fact implicated in one another. The oxymoronic 'revolutionary metaphysics' *contains* both the real and the beyond-the-real (utopian), and the image of the Fall is in fact that from an untenable position. At the same time, a critical posture is preserved, while the narrator's location in that object of criticism – society – is not denied. Hocquenghem's novels will combine social satire and observation, the beyond-the-real, and the problematising of any 'true', unimplicated position.

The one exception to this is *Les Petits Garçons/The Little Boys* of 1983, which is rather a novel of circumstances, a *roman à clef* in which the protagonists of the *affaire du Coral* of 1982–83 are thinly disguised. In what is now generally acknowledged as an attempt by elements in the police to discredit the Socialist government, an informer had alleged that sexual acts had been committed with children and other minors at a progressive institution (*lieu de vie*) in the south of France forming part of the *Collectif réseau alternatif* (Collective alternative network) run by Claude Sigala. Although some of the accusations were immediately discredited (it was clear from the outset, for example, that the culture minister Jack Lang had never set foot there), and the informer retracted and altered his statements several times, the police launched a spectacular operation, landing by helicopter and arresting Sigala and his deputy in front of the children. René Schérer, who had visited the institution for professional reasons (we recall his work on children and education), was also accused of 'excitation de mineurs à la débauche', all the time protesting his innocence. *Le Monde* in particular initially confused the 'truth' about the affair with its journalist's prejudices against the CRA and demonisation of adult–child sexual relations, and was obliged to open its columns to those intellectuals who supported Sigala and to a fuller debate about his educational methods.[2] The affair had touched Hocquenghem closely (it took some time for Schérer to clear his name), and had also disillusioned him further about the left-wing intelligentsia, many of whom had avoided getting involved in any controversy in which there was a hint of paedophilia. *Les Petits Garçons* is his immediate response, but even the *Lettre ouverte* of 1986 cannot be understood fully without reference to these events.

Clearly, the 1980s do not mark a retreat by Hocquenghem from social and political controversy. Although *Les Petits Garçons* is exceptional for one-sidedly privileging 'the real', the four other novels do not represent a flight into the aesthetic, but rather seek to understand aesthetically questions of politics, society and history, or, in the terms of *L'Ame atomique*, 'man envisaged in his aesthetic

destiny'.[3] Hocquenghem's previous writing on fiction and literature
hints at what that kind of novel might be like.

First of all, we should not expect 'gay fictions', in the sense of
texts built around stable notions of gay identity and community.
In terms now familiar, Hocquenghem in fact entitles his contribution
to the main French gay intellectual journal's balance-sheet of the
1980s, 'Where is homosexuality at in 1985? Or why I do not want
to become a "gay writer"':[4] 'The moment when literature (and its
utopia) stick to the sexual definition, they become impoverished
and mutually diminish each other.' Attentive to the real, that is
material, conditions of the literary and intellectual worlds of Paris,
he argues that we are witnessing a professional reconversion: 'For
me as a "homosexual", my whole work's direction is to avoid the
gravitation which has turned militants into booksellers, and, recip-
rocally, fashionable authors into homosexual militants.' Amid the
bitchy comments on Hervé Guibert ('a little bit of music and
artistic woolliness') and Yves Navarre ('love stories between air
stewards'), lies the serious point of Hocquenghem's rejection of
the real in the sense of the status quo ('mediocre' for everyone),
and of 'gay literature' as the vehicle for, and expression of, today's
homosexual consciousness. As he points out, since *Le Désir
homosexuel* he has been writing against 'homosexuality' in its
ghettoised, 'finished' definition.

Secondly, we should expect as readers that Hocquenghem's
novels will also break with the 'finished' and closed character of
national identity and thus of national (let alone Paris-centred)
literary traditions. In *La Beauté du métis*, Hocquenghem had
complained of the appropriation of literature by the French national
project and its participation in the official definitions of French
culture and language: 'There is no sensation of generosity in the
French novel because it always counts on the "faithful rendering"
[*le bien rendu*], and makes its goal the completion of a national and
cultural task.' The French literary tradition is largely about the
bureaucratic imposition of form and order on material in the most
author-centred and anthropocentric sense: 'the literature of the
doctors and administrators of bourgeois power as it had previously
been that of courtiers'; 'It's always a life's work, weighed down by
all the totalities of the old man from birth onwards.'[5] While there
are exceptions such as Proust, Céline and Sade, Hocquenghem cites
as examples the family genealogy of Zola's *Les Rougon-Macquart*
and the totalising project of Balzac's *La Comédie humaine*. While
there is certainly some hyperbole here, as in the rest of this work
– Hocquenghem certainly admired Balzac – the positive aspects of
foreign literary traditions are suggestive of Hocquenghem's overall
project. Tellingly, he argues that with very few exceptions French

literature throws up names of authors rather than characters (there are no French equivalents of the culturally resonant Don Quixote, Moll Flanders and Raskolnikov), and he thus valorises *enivrement* (intoxication), seduction, initiations, sensual experience. In a variation of Deleuze and Guattari's rejection of the unified and hier-archical connotations of the tree as opposed to the proliferating and heterogeneous rhizome, Hocquenghem invokes grass, 'growing between', as an appropriate image of, for example, Anglo-American literature.[6]

Thirdly, and growing out of the first two points, we should expect novels of polymorphous desire rather than novels of the self or ego. To speak the language of *L'Anti-Oedipe*, 'art, when it reaches its own grandeur, creates chains of decoding and of deterri-torialisation which inaugurate and enable to function desiring machines'.[7] This is unlike the business of forming egos in the tradition of the nineteenth-century *bildungsroman*, in which the education in life of a young person (man) is an apprenticeship of modernity itself, a process in which modernity is 'normalised' through compromise rather than the liminal, extreme or exceptional.

L'Amour en relief recounts the story of Amar, a beautiful Tunisian boy who, aged 15 in 1968, is blinded in a motorscooter accident, and Andrea, a young French psychiatric patient holidaying at the time with a group of Parisian gay men, who blames herself for the accident. The destinies of Amar and Andrea intersect in the years that follow, and the novel is narrated from their alternating points of view. Amar is adopted and seduced by a rich and old American lady of cosmopolitan origin, Mrs Halloween, who teaches him to lead an independent life. When she is killed by a truck on the Golden Gate bridge, an incident for which Andrea also blames herself, Amar is institutionalised for a year but escapes to Los Angeles, where he temporarily cohabits with a young surfer, then leads a double existence prostituting himself in West Hollywood and appearing in an act at the local Marineland as 'the blind surfer'. When he is threatened by his pimp Fatsy, he flees to the Chelsea Hotel in New York where he continues his cultural education in the Public Library and eventually joins a dance troupe that is to tour Europe. Framed by Fatsy for a drug offence in the American sector of Berlin, he is sentenced to a long term of imprisonment in the USA, but released on condition that he agrees to participate in the experiments to restore his sight conducted in Alaska by Larry, a former trick from California. A combination of helmet and cybernetic implant in the brain enables or rather forces him to see again, but when it is realised that the latter device is picking up radio trans-mitted nuclear codes, the military force him to detect the Soviet equivalents. However, the USSR sinks in her territorial waters the submarine in which they are travelling. Amar as sole survivor is captured but escapes to California where he confronts Larry in order for him to remove the implant, but Larry is accidentally killed and Amar dies in an earthquake, paroxystically receiving the broadcasts of the universe at a transmission tower. Meanwhile, Andrea has shadowed Amar's existence, falling in with his half-sisters resident in Paris as well as with a group of *gauchistes*, one of whom later helps her execute Fatsy. She is at the Chelsea Hotel during his stay but does not reveal her identity, sleeps with him once and becomes pregnant. These events alternate with her psychiatric treatment with Philippe and then Alix at his clinic near Orléans. She marries the latter and then divorces him for the alimony, to visit Amar in New York. The novel ends with a brief chapter narrated by Philippe, now cohabiting with Alix. Andrea is at the clinic, living off the money left to Mrs Halloween's cat Zita, reminiscing about the past with Amar's childhood friend Hocine, and playing with the son fathered by Amar. Amar's story had been recorded by him on a cassette machine.

Even this résumé does not do justice to the polysemy of this extra-ordinary and baroque novel, but it gives a flavour of its range and humour. It successfully juggles with two modes of writing often seen as opposites, history and fantasy, or to put it another way, realism and what we might call 'utopia-apocalypse'. The philosophical and sensual agenda, and the baroque plot, are always combined with a precise sense of time, place and milieu, be it the California or New York of the 1970s, or the University of Vincennes and the *gauchistes* of Paris. The experience of blindness, for example, is partly based on the discussions with Raul Lugo, head of an American blind gay association, whom Hocquenghem meets in New York in connection with *Le Gay Voyage*, the guidebook he writes in 1979–80.

In the space available, I shall suggest several ways into this novel, the unusual combination of which contributes to its polysemic character. It can be read as a variation of an eminent French eighteenth-century literary tradition, the *conte philosophique* or philosophical tale, explicating abstractions through narrative with Amar as the Candide figure, parodic of the picaresque novel, buffeted by events in an absurd world. The sensuousness of the text recalls a twentieth-century variation of that tradition, Sartre's *La Nausée/Nausea* of 1938. Both are novels about phenomenology, but in the case of *L'Amour en relief* this is a source of reflection about joy, desire and the workings of power rather than about existential anguish.

This novel is phenomenological in that it engages with the way reality 'appears' to us or can appear to us; it is a laboratory in which 'our' perceptual habits are disrupted in what the Russian Formalists called defamiliarisation:

'I was better than the sighted:', notes Amar, 'now I could feel the world as volumes in truly sensual depth, not pale, flat deceptive planes, but *in relief!* I could perceive the most ordinary objects in depth.'[8]

The phenomenology thus produced is of course consistent with those dynamic, atom-filled properties of space evoked in *L'Ame atomique*:

> Forces are not in depth, behind surfaces, they are at the very surface, they form the space of tensions. The particularity of surfaces is their swelling, their curving, their intrinsic power, not their flatness.[9]

Amar's escape from the normative phenomenology of the sighted also has profound political implications. As Diderot pointed out at his most materialist in the *Lettre sur les aveugles/Letter on the blind* of 1749, our sense of morality as well as our access to knowledge are dependent on our senses. Thus although Andrea's perception that Mrs Halloween's adoption of Amar is rather sinister has its own (partial) 'truth', the fact is that it does not matter that Amar is naive, just as it does not matter he is blind: he inhabits a different perceptual and moral system, sex for example is simply a way of familiarising himself with other men and women, it matters no more to him than a handshake, and completely escapes the categorisations of sexual orientation (including 'bisexuality').[10]

Amar thus also escapes, for most of the novel, the orthodoxies of a culture based on appearances or *le look*, be it among the glitterati at the thinly disguised Parisian club *Le Palace*, or, the height of irony, in the world capital of image-making, Hollywood. Moreover, from the start he rejects any of Western culture's 'explanation' of blindness as punishment, and by implication any Oedipalisation of identity,[11] as well as falling outside that Lacanian mirror stage in which the self is unified and gazes sovereign-like on to a world of perspectives.[12] Needless to say, he also thwarts that panopticism which Foucault associates with Enlightenment rationality and the construction of subjectivities characterised by interiority. The institution for blind people Amar inhabits for a year in California exemplifies the Foucauldian concept of surveillance in which the inmates never know whether they are being watched and thus always assume they are. This, and Amar's critique of Enlightenment 'philanthropy' which confined the blind to institutions, obviously also suggests the segregations implied in 'homosexual' 'identity'. Instead of devoting himself to braille (whose origins in military code work are underlined), Amar prefers dispersal out of the ghetto: 'I prefer to spend hours decoding a secret of the sighted than learning a language created for the sole use of my counterparts;' [*semblables*][13] 'I was sure of being not a blind man but an invisible voyeur of the sighted world.'[14]

Amar is thus a cyborg and a nomad. The former term, as argued by Donna Haraway in her attempt to evoke the possibilities for feminist politics of the new technologies and the subjectivities they imply, designates a hybrid of machine and organism, a self that does not end at the skin, affinity rather than identity: 'The cyborg is a kind of disassembled and reassembled post-modern collective and personal self.'[15] This new self, which 'feminists must code', is one that breaks from the centred unity associated with Western concepts of 'Man', and thus eschews narratives of unity and innocence lost when faced with contemporary 'alienation'. From the first tape recorder given him by Mrs Halloween, Amar extends himself, through Zita the cat and also through various gadgets, the most notable of which is the Optacon device at the New York Public Library which conveys printed texts and images through the feeling of touch directly on his body.[16] Haraway is clearly influenced by *L'Anti-Oedipe*, whose notion of nomadism – free movement in exteriority, limitless conductivity, open-endedness – is brought to life in Amar's journey and in the writers admired by Deleuze and Guattari such as D.H. Lawrence and Jack Kerouac: 'men who know how to leave, to scramble the codes, to cause flows to circulate, to traverse the desert of the body without organs. They overcome a limit, they shatter a wall, the capitalist barrier.'[17]

However, Amar's sense of dispersal turns out to have its fair share of ambiguity. The same America which allows him constantly to reinvent himself is also the source of those legal, technological and military powers which seek to confine him. The cybernetics of the vision prosthesis – 'A hybrid being, an electromagnetic being, was being born in me' – are to do with power, not aesthetics.[18] The Enlightenment is critiqued but also, in his reading of Western culture in New York, enables that critique even as it constructs for him an interiority. And at his death he cannot tell whether the noises in his head are the music of the spheres or the soundtrack of a science-fiction film shown on local TV.

L'Amour en relief has been criticised for its underestimation of Amar's Arab and Tunisian identity, and for thus falling into the very European tradition of using such a figure as a sounding-board, erotic or otherwise, for the author's philosophical or political preoccupations. In addition, the figure of Andrea needs to be carefully assessed, as although her narrative voice takes up roughly half the novel she is subordinated to Amar both thematically and narratively, as the preceding discussion has illustrated, and thus has a 'restricted sociosexual economy'.[19] While there is some truth in the fact that Amar's *specifically Tunisian* identity is forgotten, this is simply consistent with Hocquenghem's rejection of nationalism. The portrait of Amar is, however, not Eurocentric, as the novel is concerned to problematise severely such certainties, while simultaneously retaining an ambiguous relationship to the Enlightenment.

Since this novel is concerned to deconstruct and disperse identity, it is more appropriate to regard Amar's 'Arabness' as a strand or pathway that is culturally and thematically affirmed and surpassed. In a rare moment of self-definition, he in any case declares himself to be an American Arab – more resonant of protean possibilities – rather than a European Arab,[20] but even this is provoked and even shaped by the fact that he is justifying himself *vis-à-vis* the legal institution of the American jury that convicted him. When he renders equivalent his biological mother and Mrs Halloween in the events of his birth and rebirth, this is part of the novel's anti-Oedipal, anti-identity and even anti-anthropocentric discourse. At the same time, he does not forget the cultural inheritance of his childhood, be it the verses of the Koran or the Arab poetry and literature he consumes at the library. The colonial and even anti-colonial attitudes of the gay French tourists in Tunisia are mocked. The novel simultaneously sets up Amar as a sex object linked to his ethnicity, and then disperses its sensuality through his alternative phenomenology. The conjoined states of 'Arab' and 'blind' interact and qualify one another, as when a Chicano farmworker treats him differently from the white surfer boy: 'I was surprised to find that he took me for white, too, a European; our equality came from my blindness.'[21] And the worlds of Tunisia and high-tech California are structurally linked in the climactic sequence when Amar's cybernetically induced delirium and movements are compared to the dances of the *hadjis*, the earthquake to those on his volcanic island.

In comparison, the fate of Andrea might seem derisory, narratively subjugated to that of Amar in that he is the object of her desire and her quest. But of course that structure could be reversed, since although it is Amar and his narrative voice who carry the philosophical and political weight, he becomes in the quest narrative the equivalent of the princess in the castle, victim of Larry's experiments, and, in the version woven by Andrea, of the ogress Mrs Halloween. Indeed, Andrea 'journeys' just as much as Amar, and it is a journey of desire that decodes the desiring flows. Equivalences are set up between them, as when she notes that her first memory of him, silhouetted against the Tunisian sun, is 'blinding'.[22] Hers is a voice of satire with regard to the assumption of power and conformity by the former *soixante-huitards* of Paris. When she does eventually have sex with Amar, it is after a period in which she has been the voyeur, the gender inequality undermined – for her – by the fact she is sighted and he is not (a process reminiscent of the

Chicano's relationship with Amar): 'he's barely a man because he doesn't have a piercing stare: he's a man without defense, without attack'.[23] The parallels run to their respective experiences of the medical institution: Philippe's Oedipalising theories have no purchase on her case, and are satirised; Alix's clinic at Lamorne (poking gentle fun at Félix Guattari's La Borde) also proves inadequate; and the final narrative by Philippe exposes itself as incapable of totalising the novel's discourses. His surveillance of Andrea is balanced by the fact she has got much of what she wanted: Amar's child, a comfortable financial arrangement, and the hint she may be in touch with the cosmic radio waves of Amar's soul.

The real ambiguities of *L'Amour en relief* lie, beyond its successful interplay of realism and utopia-apocalypse and history and fantasy, in the relationship between identity and flux. This is illustrated in Amar's acceptance and even joy at the dispersal of the self implied in the absence of a position for him as spectator:

> I wasn't trying to find the 'little man' sitting back behind the window of my eyes, or inside my head. My brain ... was only a relay, a tap, an element of the earth linked to the sensitive world by intricate multiple exchanges, a mosaic of highly refined tension that no single comprehensive centre could trace ...[24]

and in drug-taking, the limit-experience of this dispersal.[25] Nevertheless, Amar's 'ego' is sufficiently formed for him to learn from his experiences, notably with the military, and for the novel to change from a chance-led *roman-feuilleton* or serial novel[26] to a quest-led narrative in the search for Larry. Amar's and Andrea's narrative voices do organise texts of centred if playful and unconventional consciousnesses, and even if neither or both constitute an overall 'truth', they have a different status from the bathetic narrative by Philippe in the closing pages. This contrast between identity and flux is lived by Hocquenghem in that between the theorist of desire and the engaged, Sartrean intellectual filling the role of the eighteenth-century *philosophe* challenging the orthodoxies of power. This theoretical problem is partly addressed in *L'Ame atomique,* with its aestheticised combination of dispersal, criticism, and utopia. *L'Amour en relief* manages to combine the cult of the sensuous particular, the evocation of a society that produces knowledge about it, and the forcing of limits beyond which the binarised categories of particular and universal dissolve. Hocquenghem as novelist is closer to Balzac than the barbs of *La Beauté du métis* might suggest. Balzac's omniscient third-person narration, with its extended and intricate knowledge of private lives and motivations, and thus of civil society (a device avoided for the dissident knowledges of *L'Amour en relief*), is nonetheless implicated in a society of anonymous, superindividual forces. In the Paris of the *Comédie humaine*, everything is unstable, all meaning is about becoming rather than being. Identity and flux coexist and are interdependent. For both Balzac and Hocquenghem, the world is one not of work and production, but of consumption, needs and desires. The clue to the ambiguities of Hocquenghem's first novel lies in the fact that the 'desiring subject' was in fact 'the new human type generated by the capitalist metropolis, and ... has always remained in syntony with it'.[27]

Hocquenghem was diagnosed HIV-positive in 1985. His fourth novel, *Eve*, is his 'AIDS novel'. This phrase arouses certain expectations. It is possible to raise certain general issues surrounding the corpus of literary works about the epidemic and the cultural debates it has aroused. Susan Sontag has warned of the dangers of metaphorising the disease, of making it stand for certain cultural and political preoccupations. What is more, the way the disease was figured in Western discourses in the 1980s means that it has engaged 'identity' as an issue, a disease of the 'Other', supposedly not affecting straight white middle-class men, with its African 'origins' and high incidence among male homosexuals and intravenous drug users. As Lee Edelman has argued,[28] the disease has raised, particularly in dominant discourses in the United States, anxieties about mastery and self-mastery, in the 'feminisation' of masculinity implicit in gay anal sex, and in the context of the decline of empire. Much of the cultural output in the USA provoked by the disease is thus a highly politicised response to the political context of the Reagan–Bush years and the continued viciousness of the Christian right.

In France, the more relaxed but in some cases equally neglectful political context, the less developed civil society and hence gay or activist 'community' (ACT-UP was founded in Paris only in 1989) arising from the republican tradition prioritising the individual–state relationship, have all meant that the cultural output has been characterised largely by personal dramas of existential choice, as in Cyril Collard's film *Les Nuits fauves/Savage Nights*, or of autobiographical dilemma. Thus Hervé Guibert's *À l'ami qui ne m'a pas sauvé la vie/To The Friend Who Did Not Save My Life* (1990) and *Le Protocole compassionnel/The Compassion Protocol* (1991) seek to avoid the fixities of 'homosexual identity' and the problematic 'confession' of his illness, complicating an autobiographical project of self-presentation which consequently depends on temporal and structural irregularity: present journal and past narrative alternate, the unspeakable end-point of the narrator's own death meaning that the project as such is never complete.

Hocquenghem shares some of Guibert's perspectives, such as an aversion to identity politics, and a Foucauldian view of the scopic power of the medical institution. However, his distaste for confessing the illness went as far as a refusal of public disclosure, a decision that might seem surprising to Anglo-Saxon readers as well as in the light of his public role in gay politics of the 1970s. His view was that to confess the nature of his illness was not equivalent to a 1970s' 'coming out', as the latter represented a political demand, whereas the disease represented chance and destiny. (Jean-Paul Aron's *Mon Sida/My AIDS* of 1987 was also a confession of homosexuality.) He thus refused a label that would set him apart and which could be used as a limiting interpretative grid.[29] Perhaps Amar's description of his condition in *L'Amour en relief* provides a clue: 'I am not a militant for blind rights and I don't wish to demonstrate how oppressed we are. Being blind is mere accident, insignificant: a purely individual quirk.'[30]

While in *Eve* the issue of AIDS is not skirted, the novel represents a startlingly distinct project. Adam Kadmon, an ironic and disabused fortyish gay Parisian novelist of Argentinian origin, encounters in the metro what he perceives as his double, in a younger version. Introduced to him by their mutual Irish-American friend Boy, this turns out to be his niece Eve, who has supposedly been imprisoned by the Communist government in Afghanistan for several months, and who is the daughter of his lesbian feminist sister Anne, whom they visit in the countryside near Bourges. It turns out that Anne's live-in lover is Judith, who had previously been infatuated with Adam, and who surprises Adam and Eve having sex. It is at this point in the narrative that Adam learns he is HIV-positive, but Eve is not infected. Adam and Eve continue their relationship and stay in the Caribbean for a year, but they have to flee when Eve kills Boy as he threatens them with a gun. They visit Adam's mother and the locations of his childhood in Buenos Aires and Uruguay, taking up with Seth, a black member of an obscure spiritual sect, with whom they form a *ménage à trois* and flee to Senegal, pursued by what Adam thinks are Boy's relatives, and then back to France. Adam's condition worsens and he is hospitalised. The truth emerges about Adam and Eve's origins. Adam's mother had been impregnated with an egg from a Nazi genetic project. It is Judith who had been impregnated with the same genetic material, giving birth to Eve in May 1968, helped by a medical student she slept with, the Dr Samael who is now treating Adam. Eve had been involved in drug-running with Boy, the real reason for her imprisonment, for their being pursued, and for the outlandish itinerary. Adam dies just as Eve is giving birth to their son, Adam.

On one level, this is a genetic version of *L'Ame atomique* (the last lines describe Adam's soul leaving his body to inhabit the new

Adam), in which we are all aleatory particles of the vast trans-historical bank of human chromosomes, with science used to back up aesthetics: 'that eternal life of which his body had been but a provisional host, the apparent phenotype, that line of genes which stretched out before him and would afterwards continue, royally indifferent, immortal, insensitive'.[31] Indeed, the text of the novel is followed by an epilogue in which Hocquenghem seeks to justify details of his narrative, including the existence of identical twins of different sexes, on scientific grounds. Parents, and Oedipalisation, are dispensed with. In *Co-ire*, Hocquenghem and Schérer had argued that genetics in fact indicated that a child was no more linked to its parents than a dictionary to a particular text.[32] In the same work, they argue that twins represent a break with the mother–child duality by providing another unity with the brother or sister. This is all in the name of the non-anthropomorphic multiplicity of the child's flows and desires across surfaces, and they thus differ from the famous portrayal of the twins in Michel Tournier's *Les Météores* (1975), in which a limit or frontier is placed between the interior-ity of Jean-and-Paul and the world, and being a twin (*la gémellité*) is a question of belonging, as if to a church or sect. Hocquenghem and Schérer argue that we all share this condition and 'possibility of perceiving the whole world, in nomadic repetition, according to an everywhere productive *gémellité*'.[33] One of the questions to be asked of *Eve* is to what extent this all-inclusiveness is preserved.

The discourses of *Eve* are conditioned by dilemmas sharpened by the cultural construction of representations of AIDS. The harsh realism of Adam's agony in the final section, at the borders of the representable, serves as that element which the text's other operations work to redeem. In Guibert's *À l'ami qui ne m'a pas sauvé la vie*, AIDS disrupts the workings of linear time: the narrator's ageing is accelerated, while at the same time he is returned to childhood with its diminished physical powers. The result is a baroque shaping of experience, a narrative of catastrophe rather than progress. Coupled with the avoidance of the metaphorisation of the disease and of its fixed symptomatic significations in medical discourse, the return to childhood and the process of dying can come to represent times before and beyond personalisation, socialisation and language. In *Eve*, Adam's relationship with Eve and then finally with his son is one of time cheated, a renewed contact with his youth, at the same time as, textually, it renews him as a writer. All through *Eve*, Adam has been contemplating a novel, first of all about Anne ('The work of my exhausted mind was again to produce, with forceps, a new reason for writing'),[34] and by the end it has taken the form of the novel (those sections narrated by him) we have just read.

This creative aspect of the discourse of *Eve* in terms of literature and also science links with that other strategy for sidestepping

linear time and causality, the level of myth. Here the most obvious
reference is to the Book of Genesis ('Adam Kadmon' is also the
primordial man in kabbalistic myth), with a similar cast of characters,
the expulsion from the Eden of the Caribbean due to Eve's duplicity,
the forbidden fruit of drugs, and a flood (in Uruguay). However,
whereas Genesis has been mobilised on the Christian right in the
USA as a master text for heterosexism and homophobia (gibes about
'Adam and Steve'), as well as a foundation for the assertion of male
mastery and subjectivity at the expense of the female, in *Eve* the
myth is reworked so that Eve not only both survives and gives birth
– painlessly – to Adam, but also participates in a Nativity and
Passion, whether as the Virgin Mary[35] or, twinning the 'crucified'
Adam as Christ,[36] the product of parthenogenesis. Moreover, in
the Gnostic tradition, Eve (or Sophia) is the creator of the world,
as one of those aeons or eternal powers emanating from the Supreme
Being who fell to Earth, creating it and the evil demiurge Samael.
She awakens Adam to knowledge only to be pursued from Eden
by the demiurge, teaching humanity that the only way to reach the
real God is through destruction and apocalypse.[37] It is in this way,
and this way only that the events of the novel can be understood
to allegorise AIDS, not as divine punishment, but as part of the
failure of the linear progress of modernity, and thus as part of a
temporality of catastrophe, 'plagues' that affect not only Adam but
also the elm trees around Anne's home.[38]

In addition, the Adam/Eve twinning partakes of the myth playfully
articulated by Aristophanes in Plato's *Symposium*, in which human
beings are the result of the gods cutting their predecessors in half
'like eggs are cut with a hair',[39] everyone now seeking the lost half
to be complete: hermaphrodites the opposite sex, while the males
seek males and the females females. Eve is the symmetrical
complement to Adam in terms of youth and gender, 'Mirror of my
femininity, of the female part of myself.'[40] The satire of the feminism
of the 1970s, expressed in the portraits of Anne and especially Judith,
is based therefore on its separatism and not on misogyny.

However, in this novel the articulation of myth and fantasy sits
less comfortably with the realist evocation of social and historical
developments, given the political urgencies of the epidemic. The
desire between Adam and Eve is strictly narcissistic, and we recall
Hocquenghem's argument in *Le Désir homosexuel* concerning the
role of narcissism in the organisation and limiting of polymorphous desire into object choice. So although Adam and Eve do have
sex together with Seth, and their relationship is 'transgressively' coded
as incest more than heterosexual, the novel emphasises a relation
between persons, an annihilation of separate personalities which
nonetheless forms a whole, in a way which seems to assert a frontier
between them and the world. Their relationship is a version of that

romantic fantasy to be found in popular culture, that impossible
sexual relation described by Lacan as the fantasy of another person
occupying your own subject position.[41] Apart from Seth and to a
certain extent Anne, everyone else in the novel is despised, and so
there is no dialectical overcoming of the antagonism between the
traditional family (half envied by Adam at the beginning) and the
solitary forty-something gay man, other than the mirroring image
of Eve and the flitting genetic or atomic particle. What is more,
Adam believes with his illness he is paying for his past sex life,[42]
and implicitly accepts the socially dominant incongruity of homosexuality and parenthood.[43] We are far from the period of *La
Dérive homosexuelle* of the 1970s, when Hocquenghem rejected, in
the name of 'plural perversity', the search for the 'âme soeur' or
soulmate,[44] or that of the FHAR, when he condemned the reductive
use of genetics in the attempts to pinpoint the 'cause' of homosexuality.[45] Indeed, Adam emphasises the power of genetics to
overcome cultural difference, while, admittedly, simply down-
grading the role of the environment as non-exclusive.[46]

The complicating factor here is that of the extreme unreliabil-
ity of the various first-person narrators, Bob the barman in the Virgin
Islands, Eve, and Adam himself, who before he knows his true
genealogy and thinks his father was an Egyptian Jew, is convinced
he sees his resemblance in old family photos. In order for such ambiguities to work, to suggest possibilities as in *L'Amour en relief*, the
novel would need the coherence that might be provided by some
kind of purchase on the power structures which crucially condition
the meanings of the epidemic (even in the case of the hospital and
Dr Samael, the latter's genetic meddling is responsible for Eve's
conception). Thus the dangers to be found in the unfolding of those
other strategies of non-causal, non-linear narration, Adam's dreams
in which he is 'punished' by Islamic fundamentalists and in which
a *fouriériste* utopian community, reminiscent to an extent of the New
York saunas evoked in *Le Gay Voyage*, is wiped out by an epidemic,
are not directly challenged. With *Eve*, Hocquenghem seems to miss
the opportunity of coherently (while still playfully) representing and
exploring the tragedies and possibilities of the 1980s, in the AIDS
epidemic but also the progressive severing of the ideological link
between heterosexuality and reproduction.

In contrast, both *La Colère de l'agneau* and *Les Voyages et aventures
extraordinaires du frère Angelo* are historical. The first, astonish-
ingly, given the subject-matter of Hocquenghem's first two novels,
is an account of the life of St John, its title a quotation from the
latter's apocalyptic visions in the Book of Revelations. Originally
an *ouvrage de commande* from the publisher Albin Michel, *La Colère*

de l'agneau grew into a vast novelistic reconstruction of the societies of the first century AD which becomes a vehicle for many of Hocquenghem's preoccupations with modernity, history, culture and power.

The life of John is recounted by his scribe Prokhore, born illegitimate to an Egyptian mother in the Jewish and Greek-speaking community of Alexandria, and pupil of Philo. After fleeing the anti-Jewish riots in the city in 38 AD, he joins John in Jerusalem, and faithfully accompanies him on his journeys until his death in Antioch in 96 AD. The bulk of the novel takes the form of a series of epistles written on John's death from Prokhore (in English, Prochor) to Clement, head of the Church, with third-person narration alternating with first-person memoirs. The period of Christ's preaching and crucifixion is the only part which Prokhore did not witness, and is narrated according to tradition (Hocquenghem bases it on John's Gospel) without commentary from Prokhore. The two men then traverse a century in which the pagan and Jewish traditions suffer world-historical setbacks, while the early Christian Church is first riven by the dispute between the Greek, cosmopolitan Paul and the apocalyptic, Jewish-mystical John. It is in order to challenge Paul's version of Christianity that John and Prokhore follow in his footsteps first to Ephesus then to Rome, where some Christians are provoked into setting fire to the city in 64 AD. Nero's anti-Christian terror produces the martyrdom of Peter and then Paul, and John is left for dead after a spectacular slaughter in the arena. John and Prokhore flee to Patmos, where John sees his apocalyptic visions, and they then witness the destruction of the Temple in Jerusalem in 70 AD before settling in Antioch.

Clearly, Hocquenghem is less interested in Christ than in the historical and cultural context. As in *L'Amour en relief*, philosophical issues are combined with the evocation of the sensuous particulars of the world: both novels are exercises in that conjunction, that mapping. This is not a secularised version of the Gospels as in, for example, Denys Arcand's film *Jésus de Montréal*, but a historicist entering into the discourses of the time, with Hocquenghem's classical erudition on full display. *La Colère de l'agneau*'s narrative sweep and breathtaking evocations of, especially, Alexandria and Rome, are a remarkable achievement. This exercise in mapping has several consequences for the twentieth-century reader. It offers a means of thinking outside modernity, but also offers tantalising similarities. The first-century AD is both different (non-rational, non-national, non-individualistic) and the same (cosmopolitan, catastrophic, innovative). Multi-ethnic Alexandria and dissolute Rome bear many resemblances to the cities evoked in Hocquenghem's *Le Gay Voyage*,[47] and this very fact disrupts neat periodisations such as 'antiquity' and 'modernity', and thus historical linearity itself.

This uncertainty, this hovering between similarity and difference, is characteristic of most historical reconstructions, be it in the form of the novel or the film and television costume drama, because of the gap between the enunciatory 'present' and the enunciated past. Homi Bhabha has described the way in which national texts construct a split between on the one hand the representation of the past as authentic, pre-given, with 'the people' as pedagogical objects, and on the other hand the performative appeal to, or inter-pellation of that 'people' to elaborate and continue those truths and values.[48] In *La Colère de l'agneau*, it is one of 'the West''s central authenticating narratives, the combination of Christianity and Roman institutions favoured here by Paul and eventually accepted by Prokhore, which is thrown into disarray.

This is where the figure of John is so crucial. The novel suggests other lineages which might have fared differently in this decisive century, notably the supremely syncretic Gnostic tradition emerging out of the cultural hybridity of Alexandria (Philo was a Hellenic Jew), and represented for example by Simon Magus. But Christianity is in itself a syncretism of the complex Mediterranean world. John is also torn between two traditions, the Hebrew and the Greek, on the one hand the apocalyptic Old Testament (the last section of the New, Revelations, in fact harks back to the Old) and the observance of Jewish Law (the initial disputes with Paul centre on the question of circumcision), and on the other, the interiorisation of belief and moral code represented in the Gospels. Far from a closed and totalised mysticism, these contradictions generate doublings, in the relationship between John and Prokhore, in doubt (John on his deathbed flirts with Gnostic beliefs), and in hope. As Hocquenghem points out in his afterword, John, unlike Paul, never accepts the world as it is, and against the early Church's institu-tional dogma and morality, and despite the rigours of his Jewish inheritance, asserts 'love, death and resurrection, flesh and spirit, light and water. John makes each of us participate in a vast poetic and metaphorical upheaval consisting of hatred and insane hope, a kind of great embolism of love.'[49] It is this excess which is put to use and to an extent tamed by Prokhore's account in his con-tribution to the construction of the edifice of the Church.

While all this may seem far removed from *Le Désir homosexuel* and even *L'Ame atomique*, many motifs and preoccupations familiar from Hocquenghem's other works can be found in the crevices of this text, a text of desire abundant in sensuous detail and striking vignettes, and they contribute to that play of uncertainty between the similarity and difference of the past. Thus there are the public latrines of Rome, shocking to the Jewish tradition, in which defecation is a collective and even social act; the unstated homo-eroticism of the disciple relationship and of John's affection for the

beautiful adolescent Gaulish prince Florin; the fleeting presence
of the Greek boys 'of bad mores'[50] at the public baths of Ephesus.
A more sustained reflection links the cities of empire in *La Colère
de l'agneau* to the arguments at the end of *L'Ame atomique* concerning
the nation. Hocquenghem and Schérer favour empires over nations,
aspire to the *fouriériste* utopia discussed in the previous chapter, but
in the end prefer a despotic empire to a despotic nation:

> States know only collectivities that are provincial, syndical,
> familial, etc. Whereas the Empire knows individuals, contenting
> itself with the smallest, molecular administrative unit at the same
> time as it realises the greatest cosmic unity.[51]

Noting the eighteenth-century's fascination with ancient empires
even as nation-states were being constructed (the example of
Edward Gibbon), Hocquenghem and Schérer's empire as phantasmagoria represents an aestheticisation of politics. This argument
again negates the Hegelian view of progress from the Roman
empire to enlightened nation-states. Of course the character of Nero
in *La Colère de l'agneau* severely problematises this argument.
Rather than the ostentation of his orgies and games creating 'a
common and peaceful surface, in the sovereign, of projection of
desires', thus guaranteeing 'peace, prosperity and civic rights',[52]
he comes to exemplify Deleuze and Guattari's body of the despot,
Foucault's description in *Surveiller et punir* of pre-Enlightenment
law inscribing itself on bodies (of the sovereign and the lawbreaker),
and the insidious relationship between desire and political oppression.
But the extraordinary *mise en scène* of the games in which the
Christians are punished also recalls the aesthetic analysis of Nero
as melancholic, originally the argument of Kierkegaard in the essay
'Equilibrium between the Aesthetic and the Ethical' in *Either/Or*,
and taken up by Hocquenghem and Schérer in *L'Ame atomique*.
Here Nero's 'hysteria of the spirit', his externalisation of the self,
his melancholy, are part of the exhaustion with the immediacy of
the world and an aspiration to something higher, 'the personality
wants to be conscious of itself in its eternal validity'.[53] Thus anxiety
is located at the heart of power, and the infinite in the immediate:

> He is without limits and incapable of understanding [or appre-
> hending] himself [...] He who subjugates and possesses is
> himself possessed and subjugated ... For all seduction comes,
> not from power really held, but from a melancholic impotence
> which delivers the master up to the desires of the crowd.[54]

Nero is thus forced by the crowd at the arena to spare Florin.

Les Voyages et aventures extraordinaires du frère Angelo deals with
another defining century, the sixteenth. Born in San Gimignano

in 1508 to republican merchants from Florence, Angelo grows up in Assisi and becomes a Franciscan novice at 14. On the fundamentalist wing of the order, he participates in the defence of Rome in 1527 by the papal forces, and witnesses its sack by the troops of the Emperor Charles V. Realising the universality of the latter's project after the siege of Florence, he participates in the imperial attack on Tunis, and saves Cortés from death. Arriving in Mexico in 1537, he becomes tutor to Francisco/Itzcoatl, son of the former Aztec Emperor Moctezuma, whom he accompanies in exile on the remote River Plate. Francisco is poisoned by the Spanish Captain who wants his treasure, and Angelo is blamed, having been caught *in flagrante* with the local sorceress. Angelo is brought back to Rome and burned at the stake for heresy. Much of the narrative is recounted through the exchange of letters between Angelo and his childhood friend Annibal, son of Spanish Jewish refugees, who in contrast to Angelo's religious zeal devotes himself to art, attaining, after a brief period of slavery in Tunisia, wealth and status in the courts of Italy.

The echoes of, in particular, *La Colère de l'agneau* are clear. The narrative sweeps through an apocalyptic century and its empires, with cities destroyed, plague, ethnocide. The competing discourses of the epoch are mobilised to map out that reality, to think not only beyond modernity, but to investigate its origins. Moreover, it is a century in which the previous structures of belief have been profoundly destabilised, in the propositions of Martin Luther, in the implications for religion of the New World, and in the new rigidities of the Counter-Reformation. In these circumstances, there emerges once again the relationship between catastrophe and utopia, the non-linear and non-progressive tide of history, and the hope suggested through apocalypse and destruction. Thus for Angelo, the New World is that promised land evoked by Thomas More:

> that dream of equality, of evangelical poverty, which these natural people seem to have anticipated; there lacked one crowning glory to their simple, patriarchal lives which know not money nor wage labour and where no ambition is manifest: the knowledge of true faith.[55]

What is more, the New World announces 'the end of the world we have known', but to Angelo's early ingenuousness, this is because 'beginning and end touch' since the Church being built there reconnects with the simplicity of the early Church.[56] In the colonial Other, Angelo finds, to his perplexity, Eden. Unlike the Moslems, the 'Indians' cannot be held responsible for their ignorance of Christ, but like at Tunis, Angelo knows already that conversion is possible only by establishing common ground between beliefs,

'then to anchor true faith in the ocean of doubt'.[57] His experiences
relativise his adherence to European civilisation and its cruelties,
and even his faith. This is announced in the prelude that begins
the novel's narrative, an account of a ceremony among the Guarani
in the River Plate area, in which a girl will eat parts of her magician
father in order to acquire his powers. This not only announces
Angelo's destiny even before he is born, but functions as equivalent
to the ceremonies in Florence evoked in the following section. In
an echo of Montaigne's famous essay, Francisco counters Angelo's
horror at the notion of cannibalism by pointing out the Eucharist
as equivalent.[58]

Tzvetan Todorov, in his study of the Spanish conquest of
Mexico,[59] points out the two elementary figures of alterity which
tended to operate: difference-inequality, in which the Mexicans were
perceived as different and therefore inferior, the logic of slavery and
massacre; and equality-identity, in which they are the same and
therefore to be assimilated to the empire and to Catholicism.
Angelo's reflections from an early stage include a chink in this binary
system: 'No, the Indian is not yet our equal. He is at the same time
more and less so: more by the simplicity of his mores and heart,
less by the ignorance of the Gospels.'[60] This process, which risks
turning out to be a variation of the misrecognition of the 'noble
savage' prevalent later in European thought, is complicated by his
encounters with the hybrid figure of La Malinche, the famous
Mexican consort of Cortés, and with the Spanish prelate who
defended the Indians, Bartolomé de Las Casas, and by his closeness
with Francisco who evokes his civilisation before the conquest. It
is intensified through desire. The diffuse desire of *La Colère de
l'agneau* is suggested in Annibal's young affection for Angelo, the
awakening of Angelo's senses in the New World as he gazes at the
native schoolboys in his charge, and of course in the sex with the
sorceress that leads to his downfall. She is Eve, close to pre-
lapsarian innocence;[61] under the effects of hallucinogenics, he
imagines her to be an animal: 'that night in which Good and Evil
merged, the eruption of his desire crossed all barriers'.[62] The
upheavals of the century and the mobility of empire have meant
that Angelo is not only cosmopolitan, but is becoming the Other.

This slippage of identity and dogma is of course punished. One
feature of this novel, which Hocquenghem anticipated would be
his last work, is the way it draws together motifs from his other works
and even life. These are to be found not only in the echoes of *La
Colère de l'agneau*, with Charles V as the new Caesar and Las Casas
comparing the conquistadors' sack of Mexico with the actions of
Nero,[63] but also in the references to Adam and Eve, in the setting
in the River Plate region as in one chapter of *Eve*. Moreover, it is

not difficult to see in Angelo's destiny, in this century of plague,[64] a certain reading of Hocquenghem's own. He was referred to by some elements in Paris as the 'angel', because of his appearance and also his incorruptibility.[65] Annibal, himself an opportunist, addresses Angelo in his last letter thus:

> Saint Angelo, you were doubtless a man of the past. Your militant, wild Faith is that of centuries gone by. It is what has caused your downfall in these new times of sceptical hypocrisy. And yet your Truth is also eternal; eternal, the struggle between purity and accommodating to the world ... you were not made for this period of order, nor for the spirit of science which accompanies and contradicts it. Your revolt was not that of our experimentalist moderns, but that of the Christian of the first centuries.[66]

Of course it would be crass to read one-to-one correspondences between Angelo and the agnostic Hocquenghem, particularly as Angelo's fate is several times compared to that of Christ (indeed Annibal explains in the last paragraph of the book that his new painting of the Passion will figure Angelo's resemblance). As with *La Colère de l'agneau*, Angelo's story partakes of an uncertain relationship of similarity and difference *vis-à-vis* the past. The sixteenth century is not the Paris of the 1980s, but since Hocquenghem does not believe in linear history but catastrophic time (a notion appropriate to recent history), and adheres to a belief in certain recurring structures, it is not altogether outlandish. As we shall see in the next chapter, this was not Hocquenghem's final word on these matters, for he has more to say about the future and its ever open possibilities.

5

Presence

Establishing a *bilan* or balance-sheet of Guy Hocquenghem's output is a paradoxical task. For if much French literary and cultural theory of the past thirty years has challenged the concepts of the unitary self and author so effectively as to render any enterprise resembling a 'life and works' project inherently problematic, Hocquenghem in particular strives to escape categorisation and even the imposition of unity within contradictions. This 'striving' is itself oxymoronic, in that it combines a self-conscious project with the dispersal of the self momentarily unified in that intentionality. That very contradiction is part of the project, and we have the unfolding of an infinite, spiralling, baroque proliferation of questioning and paradox.

Hocquenghem thus resembles an eighteenth-century *philosophe*, or the classic French intellectual challenging the misdeeds of the surrounding society (Diderot, Sartre), but he is also always concerned to saw through the epistemological bow supporting that defiance. *L'Après-mai des faunes* of 1974 is both an intervention in the traditional intellectual sense, and the undermining of terms such as 'commitment' on which such interventions had been based. The problem of his time lies in the fact that that epistemological crisis of moral, aesthetic and political legitimacy, as articulated in certain post-modern discourses, risked abandoning the advantages possessed by Enlightenment traditions in the critique of power and the status quo, their purchase on that 'real'. The year 1986 exemplifies Hocquenghem's approach, for it sees the publication of both the *Lettre ouverte*, with its devastating critique of the French intelligentsia, and *L'Ame atomique*, whose project is both to question the totalisations of Enlightenment traditions, and to offer ways of preserving critical thought and even a vision of living differently. If the aesthetics and utopia of the latter work have their inadequacies, it is to Hocquenghem's eternal credit that he refuses to accept the stasis, orthodoxies, relativisms and collusions with power of 'the real'.

This emphasis on the incomplete, on becoming rather than being, informs the sketch of an autobiographical project published posthumously as *L'Amphithéâtre des morts/The Amphitheatre of the Dead* and written in May–June 1988 before the gravity of his illness prevented further work. The title refers metonymically to one of the lecture theatres, where dissections take place, in the hospital where the narrator is being treated (in contrast with the 'amphithéâtre des étudiants'). The narrator speculates about the dead sitting and listening there. However, the book's subtitle, *Mémoires anticipées* or 'anticipated memoirs', indicates the temporal rather than spatial relationship which structures the work and its relationship with death. Traditional autobiography, that post-Enlightenment genre usually constructing a unified self, is in fact fraught with textual contradictions that undermine that project. First-person autobiography displays a veritable ontological gap, or a doubling, between the subject of the *énonciation* (the 'I' who is writing) and the subject of the *énoncé* (the 'I' who is the protagonist of the narrative). Hence the importance of the insistence upon what Philippe Lejeune calls the 'autobiographical pact', where the text through various authenticating strategies seeks to assert the unproblematic *identity* of author, narrator, and protagonist. In *L'Amphithéâtre des morts*, Hocquenghem chooses a point of enunciation in the future, thirty years hence when the narrator is still alive as an old man, living with a now treatable serious illness. The effect of this, more than the social and historical observations about the current generation's attitude to May 1968, is primarily textual. The 'unified self' of traditional autobiographical narration is constituted in a uchrony, a no-time that does not, and tragically cannot, exist. What is more, attention is diverted from Hocquenghem's impending death to his life. The text consists of tableaux from childhood and from Hocquenghem's early adult life before the foundation of the FHAR, dispersed moments of intensities and of becoming, such as being masturbated by the daughter of his English hosts while on a school exchange, going to the *lycée* and encountering his philosophy teacher Samuel experimenting with drugs. The memories of watching the country home of some Parisian *folles* he knew in his adolescence burn down are, atom-like, 'light as the bits of flying ash',[1] the project of this work is to trace them.

And yet, there is a consistency in the discourse of *L'Amphithéâtre des morts*, but, typically for Hocquenghem, it is about inconsistency: 'a mad desire not to be like the others, to refuse the easy life'.[2] This even has its teleology, for it is 'already' there in the childhood of his large, practical bourgeois household, and is connected with his later status as writer and homosexual. Surprisingly, the narrator, whom we problematically identify as Hocquenghem, even hints at a possible Oedipal interpretation, in that he chose the culture of his mother rather than the science of his father and brothers. Most significant is the praise of inconsistency and the 'double life':

I have never ceased living in two registers. Homosexual on the one hand, militant on the other, and later writer and invalid,

I've always had something to hide from half of my acquaintances. I like that; it's an enrichment.

The FHAR period marked a brief and fragile fusion of selves: 'some reserve must always be maintained. Total coherence [*adéquation*] (do what you say and say what you do) is a totalitarian dream.'[3]

This startling statement is open to critique on several points. It neglects the importance of the historical context (the difference between 1971 and 1988) in determining forms of self-presentation. While several pages earlier he had spoken warmly of Sartrean commitment ('to be neither a bastard nor a bourgeois'),[4] this statement not only contradicts Sartrean notions of authenticity and transparency, it disturbingly amalgamates that discourse with Nazism and Stalinism, a contemporary orthodoxy if ever there was one. The praxis of 1971 has given way to the aesthetics of the 1980s, with the risks of a dandyism which might be difficult to distinguish from any other social pose. As René Schérer points out, approvingly, in his afterword to this text, this attitude contrasts sharply with Hocquenghem's only other important text of self-revelation, the 'coming out' interview in *Le Nouvel Observateur* in January 1972.

My contention, however, is that although Hocquenghem's strengths lie in critical analysis rather than the construction of an alternative praxis or hegemony, he has much to tell us about politics and particularly gay politics. Clearly, he is at the 'universalising' rather than 'minoritising' end of the spectrum of gay discourse, where the latter sees homo/heterosexual definition 'as an issue of active importance primarily for a small, distinct, relatively fixed homosexual minority', and the former 'as an issue of continuing, determinative importance in the lives of people across the spectrum of sexualities'.[5] As Eve Sedgwick also points out, we cannot know in advance which emphasis is going to be the most appropriate and productive. Crucially, this will depend on the social and historical context. Hocquenghem in his life was able to combine the short-term exigencies of militant struggle (at least in the 1970s) with that utopian horizon which knows that 'homosexuality' is a label of modernity that is ultimately oppressive. The fact that his 'gay militancy' did not continue into the 1980s is largely explained by the contrasting political situations in France and in Britain/the USA. Without the status of 'minority' in civil society precariously won in the 1970s and the gay institutions it fostered, the AIDS emergency would have been yet more cataclysmic. And while it has been argued that French 'republican individualism' and the relative lack of a gay infrastructure are partly responsible for the high HIV infection rate in France,[6] it does not automatically follow that the

Anglo-Saxon model is the only solution and must be exported everywhere.

Hocquenghem constantly invites us to follow him beyond, and indeed well beyond, 'identity politics', not because he believes we are constantly inhabited by multiple identities and positions which qualify one another (such as those who believe in the primacy of social class), but because he does not believe in identity at all. The personal cannot be political because 'the personal' is an unacceptably restrictive category. Already in 1973 he had emphasised the *heter*ogeneity of the homosexual movements, the fact that at the very least it was a question of homosexuali*ties*: 'We do not aim at fidelity to ourselves, in an eternal self-resemblance [*du pareil à soi*].'[7] This applies to his view of his own 'self' ('I will not be similar to myself all my life, in the indefinite projection of the same acts'),[8] and to human existence in general, which is a play of energies and particles which extends beyond the purely personal and anthropomorphic. 'To be oneself' is an adage that is fundamentally not liberating and liberationist but oppressive and limiting.

In Hocquenghem's later writings he is aware of the contradiction between this rejection of identity and both his activism of the early 1970s and the dominant discourses of 'gay culture' in the 1980s. In *Gai-Pied Hebdo*, France's leading gay magazine of the time, he writes in 1987: 'There is therefore no definite, positive principle we can call "homosexuality", if we understand by that everything social and intimate beyond the sexual relationship between two people of the same sex.'[9] Gay self-assertion is a defensive move like any other, like nationalism, and thus, contrary to the arguments of *Le Désir homosexuel*, enjoys no special status, it is no more 'real' than normative heterosexual self-repressive fantasms. Where he is still interested in 'homosexuality', however, is in the way it both exists and does not exist, how it undermines the very assurance of its own concept. Its disappearing act, appearing and reappearing according to historical and social change, or to the structures of secrecy and disclosure, is its strength. It is a problem, a *cyclothymie*, that state of veering from euphoria to melancholy. One of the Indo-European roots of 'gay' denotes excess. The provisionality of 'homosexuality' implies tension rather than fulfilment or taking for granted one's position or identity. Still influenced by Foucault and Deleuze, Hocquenghem sees visibility and confession as traps, double binds of compulsory transgression that cannot be ends in themselves:

> 'Visibility' is the faculty of 'saying oneself', of being adequate to the idea of oneself, frankness, constancy of meaning, the unequivocal content of the message (gay [*homo*] and proud to be so). I was for visibility when it was emergence [*apparition*].

Today ... I find myself wishing for its disappearance. Without
a play with invisibility, visibility is no more than pointless fool-
ishness, a false problem, second-rate psychology.

This play of appearance and disappearance is ultimately aesthetic,
but the art form invoked to express it is based on sound:

I would 'musicalise' ['*musicaliserais*'] the idea of homosexuality: it exists only in its rhythm, its intervals and its pauses, it
exists only through its (dramatic) movement, It conjugates
invisibility and visibility in this rhythm of emergence and disappearance.

The intellectual references for these analogies are Leibniz, with his
concept of monads, individual entities and substances analogous
with the soul that make up the world, which is the sum of all these
points of view (thus no partial view will do); and Kierkegaard, whose
ethical self, caught between finite sensuous immediacy and the
eternity of faith, depends for its existence on tension, being 'tensed',
a ceaseless process of re-enactment and endless becoming.

This late article combines the strengths and weaknesses of
Hocquenghem's final positions on gay politics. Those familiar
with Hocquenghem only from *Le Désir homosexuel* may be disappointed at what seems here to be his political reticence. He argues
against Gay Pride marches, in that nowadays confession can be taken
as aggression of the other, and declares that the final aim is, not
of course to hide, but to be treated 'as if there were no difference'.
The discussion of appearance and disappearance may seem inap-
propriately rhapsodic, given the fact that there are those, and we
need to think only of the cultural polarisations in the United States,
who seek the literal disappearance of homosexuals. His refusal of
the concept of ideology means that he fails adequately to explain
that 'homosexuals' 'appear' when they are interpellated as such,
when homophobic laws and violence are applied and enacted.

If this text is about aesthetics and ethics rather than politics, it
nonetheless brings some fresh air to Anglo-Saxon debates. This is
not just that Leibniz and Kierkegaard make a change from psychoanalysis, but also that it reminds us of the limits of 'identity', how
interpellation can produce the reverse effect of self-assertion, but
also fixes and separates us. It is the case, for example, that many
gay men feel most 'gay' in situations where they are minoritised,
and not in the cultivated spaces of plenitude and self-affirmation.
And it is a crucial political task to ensure that the venues of, for
example, London Gay Pride – in recent years, working-class Brixton
and the East End – experience the event not as Other but as part
of their own diversity and struggles. Hocquenghem in all his work,
in fact, simultaneously provides an opening towards the universe

of possibilities, the whole of history, culture and experience, while refusing to see that 'universal' in terms of the dominant order or status quo. Being treated 'as if there were no difference' definitely does not mean assimilation to the Same. Rather, his project is to foster the inherently critical legacy and positioning of 'homosexuality', and he points out that it is the proximity and resemblance of the Other to the Same, when it is most 'unidentifiable', as with the Jews in Nazi Germany, which is the most challenging to dominant orders. A quarter of a century after *Le Désir homosexuel*, Hocquenghem still sees homosexuality as in the vanguard of a reality that is infinitely heterogeneous, ceaselessly in a process of becoming, 'becoming the Other', if we recall the vocabulary of *La Beauté du métis*. This utopian charge is crucial in the context of the necessary, but necessarily provisional, notions of identity which characterise current conflicts and may shape future successes.

If Hocquenghem is not 'gay' as such, is he 'queer'? Michael Moon's useful preface to the 1993 edition of *Homosexual Desire* hints at a teleology, with the work being read as queer theory *avant la lettre*. The polarised cultural political situation in the United States, and the desire by certain activists and academics to reinvigorate and re-radicalise the terms 'lesbian' and 'gay', are the context for the flourishing of the term 'queer' since the beginning of the 1990s. As the provocative use of the adjective suggests, 'queer' involves the defiant appropriation of the abject and a rejection of strategies of minoritised acceptance, tolerance, and petitioning for rights. It thus embraces all lesbian, gay, bisexual and other 'deviant' sexual practices not necessarily defined by object-choice, and, influenced by the post-modern, seeks to destabilise the comforting binary categories whereby gender and the homo/hetero distinction operate by referring to 'the open mesh of possibilities, gaps, overlaps, dissonances and resonances, lapses and excesses of meaning when the constituent elements of anyone's gender, of anyone's sexuality are made (or *can't be* made) to signify monolithically'.[10] This process of generalised perversity, in which desire and sexuality take precedence over gender and other constructs, can be encouraged by technology and the proliferation of cyborg culture.

Such an approach has been productive but not without its problems. There is a fundamental ambiguity at the heart of queer theory between identity and non-identity. If 'I' am queer or 'identify as queer', then identity has crept back in, and queerness becomes another, funkier form of minoritising identity politics, 'gay' with body piercing. (The tenuous link between academic queer theory and urban, often non-white activist groups such as Queer Nation is a case in point.) If the aim is to undermine binary thought, then implicitly everyone is actually or potentially queer, and it becomes a highly universalising concept. For theorists such as Judith Butler,

these ambiguities form one of the strengths of 'queer' when its per-
formativity (language use which enacts a new reality as in 'I
pronounce you man and wife', 'identity' thus as a kind of stylised
repetition) is combined with awareness of the histories of discourse
and power attached to it, so that it represents 'a discursive site whose
uses are not fully constrained in advance'.[11] In the rejection of 'traditional' 'gay' politics of rights or of hegemony construction, 'queer'
risks however being limited to an artistic avant-garde ever attentive
to the shock of the new, or to a reproduction of general capitalist
consumer relations, in which Marx's and Freud's concepts of the
fetish intriguingly merge.

Hocquenghem shares many of these priorities and ambiguities.
He rejects assimilation and the reluctance to present anything but
'positive images' to general heterosexual society. He gives preemi-
nence to desire and 'passions' rather than to persons and identities,
and consequently he has little to say about gender, but, as we have
seen, Enlightenment notions of a critical consciousness linger on.
He is wary of the discourse of rights, for good Foucauldian reasons
and in particular for its association with the liberal-national-statist
tradition born out of 1789. He seeks above all else to undermine
the bases of the 'norm'. However, he is simultaneously more
universal and more historical. At a conference on gay and lesbian
families held at the Institute of Contemporary Arts in London in
December 1994, Angela Mason of the pressure group Stonewall,
which has been vilified by some gay and queer activists for working
within the political and lobbying system, questioned the limitations
of her opponents' viewpoints by stating, as a mother herself,
'There's nothing queer about a baby.' For Hocquenghem of course
there is, and if 'queerness' is to be understood as a varying combination of sexual deviance, the polymorphous perverse and the
surpassing of binary categories, then it can be found, stimulatingly,
in the most surprising places, in *Treasure Island*, in Gnosticism, in
Nero, in a baroque church. Hocquenghem demonstrates that to
be distant from Enlightenment notions of causality and progress
does not mean to abandon history altogether, with its surprises,
catastrophes and utopianism. Transgression and deviance are part
of an unfolding and never-ending relationship with 'norms', and
this forms part of his rejection of 'compulsory transgression'.

In the end, Hocquenghem's view of sexuality is more extensive
and more *sublime*, and this is provoked by that link between
sexology, positivism and consumerism which characterised certain
aspects of 1970s' 'liberation'. One of the critiques of *Le Désir
homosexuel* in 1973 had questioned desire's – and the anus's –
non-complicity with capitalism and normality: the 'pick-up machine'
or cruising sets up binary oppositions between intellectual and
sexual stimulation and activity, and like consumerism constructs

its desires *vis-à-vis* an absence, that of the next object.[12] By 1986, Hocquenghem is emphasising 'passions', which are aesthetic, rather than 'sexuality', with its links with positivist science: the aesthetics of passions 'are not to do with any concept ... it includes the sexual, but by constantly transgressing its limits'.[13] The project of *L'Ame atomique*, as we have seen, is to reinvigorate and re-formulate, not 'deviance' as such, but the auratic and the melancholic: 'post-modernity is but a display of sex-objects from which all soul is withdrawn'.[14] In these terms, even celibacy or 'platonic' love have their roles, for they 'lift and add spice to the platitude of sensuality left to itself. The realm of the soul [*l'animique*] is the accomplice of the sensual, not its censor.'[15] The 'sublime body' is both 'spiritual flesh and fleshly spirit', the exaltation of the body, its potentialities, its becoming.[16]

Of course this approach has its blind spots. The reader of *L'Ame atomique*, cheered by this re-connection with the universal via the particular, is disappointed to read the assumption of whiteness and white skin in the discussion about childhood, colour, and dirt.[17] Hocquenghem's anathematising of feminism as some of its separatist excesses of the 1970s means that a dialogue on the fluidities and fixities of gender is never broached. The self, the anus, the sex, is never one. His preoccupation with singularities and particles means that he rarely grasps the force of the interpellations via which most people live, and perform, their imaginary relations with the real. The relevance for lesbians (as opposed to gay men) of many of his arguments is never more than implicit. Teresa de Lauretis is thus right to berate French male theorists such as Foucault and Deleuze, in their critiques of unified subjectivity and denial of gender, for ignoring 'the social relations of gender that constitute and validate the sexual oppression of women'[18] (although for her any disavowal of gender is 'ideology'). It is the force and weakness of Hocquenghem's utopianism, however, that he of course does the same for 'homosexuals'. This decoupling of the aesthetic from its role in modern society in constructing and participating in the shifts of hegemonic structures of feeling underlines the rather aristocratic dimension of his thought. Just as the Mitterrand years are unam-biguously savaged along with that active French state which they prolong and augment, despite, arguably, their role in preserving France from the excesses of 1980s' neo-liberalism and momentarily at least in the building of majorities against the *Front national*, so is Hocquenghem reluctant to enter the domain of the 'popular'. This is despite the fact that this was one of the shortcomings for which he lambasted French national culture in *La Beauté du métis*. His humour, and his refusal of the boundaries of the body, might have led him to embrace Bakhtinian carnival and its overturning of hierarchies, but for him contemporary versions of *la fête* are tainted by the hand of state power and official culture. In his novels

however, especially *L'Amour en relief* and *La Colère de l'agneau*,
erudition and philosophical speculation tend neatly to combine with
popular cultural forms. The first of these mobilises science fiction,
road movies, myths of America; the second, the sensuous spectacle
of the cinematic epic, what the French call the peplum.

Politically, Hocquenghem's refusal of the legacy of 1789 char-
acterises the dualities of his position. For the refusal is of
republicanism and egalitarianism in the name of difference and
heterogeneity, but also of social relations of oppression in the name
of true liberation. There is no hint of relativism in his works. The
Marxist tradition seeks dialectically to prise open the possibilities
of the new era associated with production, the law (a formal
equality), the nation (source of popular participation as well as official
mystification), and surpass these with a new society that builds on
the shortcomings of its predecessors. Thus careful distinction must
be made between the different legacies, fascist or democratic, of
the Enlightenment. What Hocquenghem emphasises, however, is
the way in which modern society creates neurotic, miserable individuals in a degraded relationship to themselves and the world. On
the other hand, the ludic and local resistances and positionalities
of post-modern theories are not enough, and it is in this sense that
Hocquenghem's thought is both atopic and utopian. As Andreas
Bjørnerud has argued in relation to the French specificity of that
other ambiguously gay intellectual, Roland Barthes, gay politics may
take an atopic form, in the sense of a *movement* that disturbs binary
categories. Barthes thus works within and resists, rather than looks
beyond and seeks to escape, the symbolic and cultural context. His
'coming out' shifts definitions rather than attaining a new one, and
this is appropriate, given the eminent questionability and provisionality of gay identities.[19] It has also been argued that queer theory
'points not toward a differently ordered utopia but toward a non-
conditioned and nonordered atopia'.[20] Hocquenghem's refusal of
the given includes, however, the shifting and precarious categories
of contemporary capitalist consumerism (although he provides us
with ways of imaginatively living in that society), and extends
beyond them. The advantages of Fourier's utopia lie in the fact that
its (different) 'order' is devoted to the kaleidoscopic and always
altering happiness of profoundly unstable, always incomplete, sets
and fragments of potentialities.

What is missing in Hocquenghem's thought, of course, is the
praxis, how to get there. It is this which marks him out as an imagi-
native artist rather than a social or political theoretician. His work
is incomplete in all senses, since it is about incompleteness, and it
is cut short. This introduction to Hocquenghem has sought not to
unify that life and work but to enable the articulations of his ideas
to find places in our own ongoing debates.

References

Preface

1. For a rare example of Hocquenghem's work (in particular *Le Désir homosexuel*) being put to use, see P.J. Smith, *Laws of Desire: Questions of Homosexuality in Spanish Writing and Film 1960–1990* (Oxford University Press, 1992); and '"The Captive's Tale": Race, Text, Gender', in R.A. El Saffar and D. de Armas Wilson (eds), *Quixotic Desire: Psychoanalytic Perspectives on Cervantes* (Cornell University Press, 1993) pp. 227–35.

Chapter 1: After May

1. See for example the itinerary of Bernard Kouchner, dissident member of the 'Italian' tendency in the 1960s and who later went on to become a founder of *Médecins sans frontières* and a minister of health under Mitterrand in the 1980s. See H. Hamon and P. Rotman, *Génération: les années de rêve* (Seuil, 1987).
2. For more on this point, see N. Hewitt (ed.), *The Culture of Reconstruction: European Literature, Thought and Film 1945–50* (Macmillan, 1989).
3. J. Girard, *Le Mouvement homosexuel en France 1945–1980* (Syros, 1981).
4. We should recall, however, the general homophobia of Surrealists such as André Breton.
5. A. Touraine, *Le Mouvement de mai ou le communisme utopique* (Seuil, 1968).
6. R. Aron, *La Révolution introuvable* (Fayard, 1968).
7. G. Hocquenghem, 'Pourquoi nous nous battons', *Action*, 7 May 1968; G. Hocquenghem, *L'Apres-mai des faunes: Volutions* (Grasset, 1974) p. 45.
8. Hocquenghem, *L'Après-mai*, p. 32.
9. At the time, among many Parisian students, Mao's Cultural Revolution was perceived as truly anti-bureaucratic and anti-authoritarian, and thus as avoiding the errors of Stalinism.

10. G. Hocquenghem, *Lettre ouverte à ceux qui sont passés du col Mao au Rotary* (Albin Michel, 1986) p. 124.

11. G. Hocquenghem, 'Pompidou, nous ne serons pas tes familles!', Hocquenghem, *Tout*, no. 5 (December 1970); Hocquenghem, *L'Après-mai*, p. 136.

12. J. D'Emilio, *Sexual Politics, Sexual Communities: The Making of a Homosexual Minority in the United States 1940–1970* (Chicago: University of Chicago Press, 1983) p. 33.

13. G. Hocquenghem, *La Dérive homosexuelle* (Jean-Pierre Delarge, 1977) p. 24.

14. G. Hocquenghem, 'La Révolution culturelle ne tombe pas du ciel', *Révolution culturelle*, nos 1–2 (June 1969); Hocquenghem, *L'Après-mai*, p. 49.

15. *Faire la révolution*, no. 2 (April 1970); Hocquenghem, *L'Après-mai*, p. 56.

16. G. Hocquenghem, 'Ils ne sont pas morts de vieillesse', *L'Idiot Liberté*, no. 1 (January 1971); Hocquenghem, *L'Après-mai*, p. 119. G. Hocquenghem, 'Stupéfiants: Stupéfiant!', Hocquenghem, *Tout*, no. 8 (February 1971); *L'Apres-mai*, p. 131.

17. G. Hocquenghem, 'Vive le Bengale libre', Hocquenghem, *Tout*, no. 13 (May 1971); *L'Après-mai*, p. 91.

18. Hocquenghem, *La Dérive*, p. 53.

19. G. Hocquenghem, 'Où est passé mon chromosome?', *Tout*, no. 12 (April 1971); Hocquenghem, *L'Après-mai*, p. 150; FHAR *Rapport contre la normalité* (Champ libre, 1971) p. 64.

20. G. Hocquenghem, 'Notre corps nous appartient', *Tout*, 12 (April 1971); Hocquenghem, *L'Aprés-mai*, p. 143.

21. G. Hocquenghem, 'Pour une conception homosexuelle du monde', *Rapport*, p. 73; Hocquenghem, *L'Apres-mai*, p. 159. Author's emphases.

22. Hocquenghem, *Rapport*, p. 74; Hocquenghem, *L'Après-mai*, p. 162.

23. G. Hocquenghem, *Rapport*, p. 77; Hocquenghem, *L'Après-mai*, p. 165.

24. G. Hocquenghem, 'Aux péderastes incompréhensibles', *Partisans* (July 1972); Hocquenghem, *La Dérive*, p. 52.

25. Girard, *Le Mouvement*, p. 98.

26. Ibid., p. 138.

27. Hocquenghem, *Rapport*, p. 66; Hocquenghem, *L'Après-mai*, p. 154.

28. Hocquenghem, *Rapport*, p. 74; Hocquenghem, *L'Après-mai*, p. 161.

29. Hocquenghem, *L'Après-mai*, pp. 141, 157.

30. Hocquenghem, *La Dérive*, p. 18.

31. Hocquenghem, *L'Après-mai*, p. 176.

32. Hocquenghem, *La Dérive*, p. 38.
33. Ibid., p. 57.
34. Ibid., p. 15.
35. Ibid., p. 132.
36. Ibid., p. 18.
37. Ibid., p. 17.
38. Hocquenghem, *L'Après-mai*, pp. 199–200.
39. Hocquenghem, *La Dérive*, pp. 135–8. In the *Lettre ouverte* of 1986, Hocquenghem takes completely the opposite view: Hocquenghem, *Lettre*, p. 116.
40. Hocquenghem, *La Dérive*, p. 107.
41. Ibid., p. 19.
42. Ibid., p. 140.
43. Ibid., p. 109.
44. Hocquenghem, *Rapport*, pp. 97–104.
45. G. Hocquenghem, 'Tout le monde ne peut pas mourir dans son lit', *Libération*, 29 March 1976; Hocquenghem, *La Dérive*, pp. 128–33.
46. Quoted in D. Hanley, P. Kerr, N. Waites, *Contemporary France: Politics and Society since 1945* (Routledge, 1984) p. 38.
47. P. Ory, *L'Aventure culturelle française* (Flammarion, 1989) p. 125.
48. Ibid., p. 180.
49. Ibid., p. 195.
50. Ibid., p. 225.
51. Quoted in Hocquenghem, *Lettre ouverte*, p. 15. It is worth recalling Hocquenghem's begrudging acceptance on the same page of the term 'generation' and its implications: 'I don't like the idea of belonging to this coagulated block of disappointments and fellowships, which comes into being and is perceived as such only at the time of the massive treachery of middle age. You become a generation only when you retract, like a snail in its shell.'
52. Hocquenghem, *Lettre ouverte*, p. 16.
53. It should be noted that the candidate of the other main Trotskyist group in France, Arlette Laguiller of *Lutte ouvrière*, obtained an unprecedented 5 per cent of the vote in the first round of the presidential elections on 23 April 1995.
54. Hocquenghem, *Lettre ouverte*, p. 15.
55. Ibid., pp. 32–3.
56. Ibid., p. 56.
57. Ibid., p. 72.
58. Ibid., pp. 54, 154, 180.
59. Ibid., p. 112.
60. Ibid., p. 197.
61. Ibid., pp. 37–8.

62. Ibid., p. 90.
63. Ibid., p. 100.
64. Ibid., p. 66.
65. Ibid., p. 89.
66. Ibid., p. 94.
67. Ibid., p. 177.
68. Ibid., p. 34.
69. Ibid., p. 134.
70. Ibid., p. 143.
71. Ibid., p. 17.
72. Ibid., p. 23.
73. Ibid., p. 95.
74. Ibid., p. 39.
75. Ibid., pp. 16, 46.
76. Ibid., p. 48.
77. Ibid., p. 197.
78. Ibid., pp. 118–19.
79. Hocquenghem, *L'Après-mai*, p. 202.
80. L. Joffrin, *Un Coup de jeune: portrait d'une génération morale* (Arlea, 1987) pp. 109–13.
81. R. Debray, 'A Modest Contribution to the Rules and Ceremonies of the Tenth Anniversary', *New Left Review*, no. 115 (May–June 1979) p. 48. Hocquenghem does not spare Debray in the *Lettre ouverte*.
82. P. Ory, *L'Entre-deux-mai: Histoire culturelle de la France Mai 1968–Mai 1981* (Seuil, 1983) p. 171.
83. G. Lipovetsky, *L'Ere du vide: essais sur l'individualisme contemporain* (Gallimard, 1983) pp. 50–1.
84. Ibid., p. 244.
85. Hocquenghem, *L'Après-mai*, p. 202.
86. Ibid., p. 8.
87. *La Dérive*, p. 17.
88. Hocquenghem, *L'Après-mai*, p. 193.

Chapter 2: Desire

1. G. Hocquenghem, *Lettre ouverte*, p. 93.
2. See above, p. 19.
3. L. Althusser and E. Balibar, *Reading Capital*, translated by Ben Brewster (NLB, 1970).
4. In L. Althusser, *Lenin and Philosophy and Other Essays*, translated by Ben Brewster (NLB, 1971) pp. 121–73.
5. S. Turkle, *Psychoanalytic Politics: Freud's French Revolution* (Burnett Books, 1979) p. 45.

REFERENCES99

6. G. Hocquenghem, *Homosexual Desire*, translated by D. Dangoor (Durham Duke University Press, 1993) p. 95.
7. Ibid., p. 109.
8. Ibid., p. 114.
9. S. Freud, 'Three Essays on Sexuality', in *Standard Edition of the Complete Psychological Works*, translated by J. Strachey and A. Freud, vol. 7 (Hogarth Press, 1953) p. 145. Quoted in Hocquenghem, *Homosexual Desire*, p. 75.
10. Hocquenghem, *Homosexual Desire*, pp. 121–2.
11. G. Deleuze and F. Guattari, *Anti-Oedipus: Capitalism and Schizophrenia*, translated by R. Hurley, M. Seem, and H. Lane (Athlone Press, 1984) pp. 4–5.
12. R. Braidotti, *Patterns of Dissonance: a Study of Women in Contemporary Philosophy*, translated by E. Guild (Cambridge: Polity Press, 1991) p. 67.
13. Deleuze and Guattari, *Anti-Oedipus*, p. 19.
14. Hocquenghem, *La Dérive*, pp. 77–8.
15. Deleuze and Guattari, *Anti-Oedipus*, p. 63.
16. Ibid., p. 179.
17. Ibid., p. 72.
18. J. Butler, *Subjects of Desire: Hegelian Reflections in Twentieth-Century France* (New York: Columbia University Press, 1987) p. 209.
19. Note however the critiques of Deleuze and Guattari in T. de Lauretis, *Technologies of Gender: Essays on Theory, Film and Fiction* (Macmillan, 1989) and A. Jardine, *Gynesis: Configurations of Woman and Modernity* (Cornell University Press, 1985) pp. 208–23.
20. Deleuze and Guattari, *L'Anti-Oedipe: capitalisme et schizophrénie* (Minuit, 1972) pp. 474–5. An appendix not included in the English edition.
21. Deleuze and Guattari, *Anti-Oedipus*, p. 293.
22. Ibid., p. 348.
23. Ibid., p. 260.
24. Quoted in René Schérer (ed.), *Charles Fourier ou la contestation globale* (Seghers, 1970) p. 69.
25. Deleuze and Guattari, *Anti-Oedipus*, p. 292.
26. Hocquenghem, *L'Après-mai*, p. 65.
27. Schérer, *Charles Fourier*, p. 8.
28. Hocquenghem, *Homosexual Desire*, p. 52.
29. S. Freud, 'Psychoanalytic Notes on an Autobiographical Account of a Case of Paranoia (1911)' *Standard Edition*, vol. 12 (Hogarth Press, 1958) pp. 9–82.
30. Ibid., p. 46.
31. Hocquenghem, *Homosexual Desire*, p. 84.
32. Freud, 'Psychoanalytic Notes', p. 61.

33. Hocquenghem, *Homosexual Desire*, p. 80.
34. Ibid., p. 81.
35. Ibid., p. 121.
36. Ibid., p. 131.
37. Deleuze and Guattari, *L'Anti-Oedipe*, p. 477.
38. Hocquenghem, *Homosexual Desire*, p. 141. Hocquenghem's theoretical writings on children will be discussed further in the next chapter.
39. Hocquenghem, 'Capitalism, the Family and the Anus', in ibid., pp. 93–112.
40. Deleuze and Guattari, *Anti-Oedipus*, pp. 210–11.
41. Ibid., p. 120.
42. Hocquenghem had expressed mistrust of the 'quantifying' nature of the Kinsey report, while acknowledging its historical importance.
43. Ibid., p. 88.
44. Ibid., p. 62.
45. Ibid., p. 150.
46. Ibid., p. 143.
47. Ibid., p. 133.
48. Ibid., p. 137.
49. Ibid., p. 145.
50. '"What we are talking about here", he intoned gravely, "is the putting of a penis into a man's arsehole".' See M. Simpson, 'Backs to the wall', *Time Out*, 9–16 March 1994, p. 91.
51. M. Mieli, *Homosexuality and Liberation: Elements of a Gay Critique*, translated by D. Fernbach (Gay Men's Press, 1980) p. 171.
52. Ibid., p. 216.
53. Ibid., p. 193.
54. Ibid., p. 75.
55. Ibid., p. 65.
56. Ibid., p. 32.
57. Ibid., p. 148.
58. Ibid., p. 56. My emphasis.
59. Ibid., pp. 57–8, 157.
60. Ibid., pp. 38, 54.
61. Ibid., p. 169.
62. Ibid., p. 135.
63. Ibid., p. 240n.
64. Hocquenghem, *Homosexual Desire*, p. 51.
65. Ibid., p. 55.
66. Hocquenghem, *La Dérive*, p. 20.
67. G. Hocquenghem, *Race d'Ep! Un siècle d'images de l'homosexualité* (Libres-Hallier, 1979) p. 12.
68. Deleuze and Guattari, *Anti-Oedipus*, p. xiv.

69. Mieli, *Homosexuality and Liberation*, pp. 119–20.
70. Hocquenghem, *La Derive*, p. 104.

Chapter 3: Modernity

1. G. Hocquenghem and J.-L. Bory, *Comment nous appelez-vous déjà? Ces hommes que l'on dit homosexuels* (Calmann-Lévy, 1977) pp. 88–97.
2. Ibid., p. 135.
3. Ibid., p. 149.
4. For more on this point, see L. Trilling, *Sincerity and Authenticity* (Oxford University Press, 1972).
5. Hocquenghem and Bory, *Comment nous appelez-vous déjà?*, p. 152.
6. Ibid., p. 139.
7. Ibid., p. 158.
8. Ibid., p. 180.
9. Ibid., p. 150.
10. In Michel de Certeau's work on everyday life, the *parcours* is associated with 'the microbe-like, singular and plural practices which an urbanistic system [associated with the *carte*] was supposed to administer or suppress, but which have outlived its decay': 'Walking in the City', in S. During (ed.), *The Cultural Studies Reader* (Routledge, 1993) p. 156.
11. Hocquenghem and Bory, *Comment nous appelez-vous déjà?*, pp. 165, 177, 197.
12. Ibid., p. 197.
13. See Chapter 1, 'Goethe's *Faust*: The Tragedy of Development', in M. Berman, *All That Is Solid Melts Into Air: The Experience of Modernity* (Verso, 1982) pp. 37–86.
14. Hocquenghem and Bory, *Comment nous appelez-vous déjà?*, p. 156.
15. Ibid., p. 185.
16. Berman, *All That Is Solid*, p. 19.
17. W. Benjamin, 'On Some Motifs in Baudelaire', in *Illuminations*, translated by H. Zohn (Fontana/Collins, 1973) p. 171.
18. Berman, *All That Is Solid*, p. 152.
19. Hocquenghem and Bory, *Comment nous appelez-vous déjà?*, p. 161.
20. See above, note 7.
21. Hocquenghem and Bory, *Comment nous appelez-vous déjà?*, p. 163.
22. Benjamin, *Illuminations*, p. 174.
23. Hocquenghem and Bory, *Comment nous appelez-vous déjà?*, p. 169.

24. Benjamin, *Illuminations*, p. 178.
25. Hocquenghem and Bory, *Comment nous appelez-vous déjà?*, p. 169.
26. Benjamin, *Illuminations*, p. 179.
27. Ibid., p. 190.
28. Ibid., pp. 192–3.
29. T. Eagleton, *Walter Benjamin or Towards a Revolutionary Criticism* (Verso, 1981) p. 6.
30. W. Benjamin, 'The Work of Art in the Age of Mechanical Reproduction', in Benjamin, *Illuminations*, p. 224.
31. Hocquenghem, *La Dérive*, pp. 109–20.
32. Hocquenghem and Schérer, *Co-ire: album systématique de l'enfance, Recherches*, no. 22 (1976) p. 45.
33. Ibid., p. 48.
34. Ibid., p. 55.
35. Ibid., p. 28.
36. Ibid., p. 60.
37. Ibid., p. 59.
38. See the excellent and balanced discussion in J. Weeks, *Sexuality and its Discontents* (Routledge, 1985) pp. 223–31.
39. M. Foucault, G. Hocquenghem, J. Danet, 'La Loi de la pudeur' in 'Fous d'enfance: qui a peur des pédophiles?', *Recherches*, nos 36–7 (April 1979) pp. 69–82.
40. Hocquenghem and Schérer, *Co-ire*, p. 89.
41. G. Hocquenghem, *La Beauté du métis: réflexions d'un francophobe* (Ramsay, 1979) p. 17.
42. Ibid., p. 18.
43. Ibid., p. 12.
44. Ibid., p. 15.
45. Ibid., p. 158.
46. Ibid., pp. 32, 135.
47. Ibid., p. 82.
48. Ibid., p. 117.
49. Ibid., p. 43.
50. Berman, *All That Is Solid*, p. 22.
51. B. Massumi, *A User's Guide to Capitalism and Schizophrenia: Deviations from Deleuze and Guattari* (Boston, MIT Press, 1992) p. 129.
52. A. Giddens, *The Transformation of Intimacy: Sexuality, Love and Eroticism in Modern Societies* (Cambridge, Polity Press, 1992). See for example his comments on 'autonomy' – a buzzword in Paris in May 1968 – in post-traditional societies, p. 185.
53. Mieli, *Homosexuality and Liberation*, p. 170.
54. Ibid., p. 180: 'the individualistic atomisation of the species, an atomisation that followed and replaced the gradually destroyed community'.

55. T. Eagleton, *The Ideology of the Aesthetic* (Oxford, Blackwell, 1990) p. 3.
56. Eagleton in fact writes: 'Custom, piety, intuition and opinion must now cohere an otherwise abstract, atomized social order', ibid., p. 23.
57. Ibid., p. 369.
58. G. Hocquenghem and R. Schérer, *L'Ame atomique: pour une esthétique d'ère nucléaire* (Albin Michel, 1986) p. 316.
59. Ibid., pp. 14–15.
60. Ibid., p. 27.
61. Ibid., p. 16.
62. Ibid., p. 295.
63. Ibid., p. 51.
64. Ibid., p. 280; Lucretius, *On the Nature of the Universe*, translated by R.E. Latham (Harmondsworth: Penguin, 1994) p. 32.
65. Hocquenghem and Schérer, *L'Ame atomique*, p. 21.
66. Ibid., pp. 104–5.
67. Ibid., p. 49.
68. Ibid., p. 58.
69 Ibid., p. 114.
70. Ibid., p. 22.
71. Ibid., p. 297.
72. Ibid., p. 23.
73. Ibid., p. 85.
74. Ibid., p. 156.
75. S. Plant, *The Most Radical Gesture: The Situationist International in a Postmodern Age* (Routledge, 1992) p. 86.
76. Hocquenghem and Schérer, *L'Ame atomique*, p. 140. The themes of doubling and secrets, and of confession, are developed in a volume Hocquenghem co-edited with the journalist Jean-Luc Hennig, based on their radio phone-in programme 'Il suffit de dire': *Les Français de la honte: la morale des Français d'aujourd'hui racontée par eux-mêmes* (Albin Michel, 1983).
77. Hocquenghem and Schérer, *L'Ame atomique*, p. 158.
78. Ibid., p. 168.
79. S. Heath, 'Narrative Space', in *Questions of Cinema* (Macmillan, 1981) pp. 19–75.
80. Hocquenghem and Schérer, *L'Ame atomique*, p. 96.
81. Ibid., p. 113.
82. Ibid., p. 106.
83. Eagleton, *Ideology of the Aesthetic*, p. 90.
84. Hocquenghem and Schérer, *L'Ame atomique*, p. 240.
85. Ibid., p. 232.
86. Ibid., p. 332.
87. Ibid., p. 316.
88. Ibid., p. 326.

89. R. Barthes, *Sade, Fourier, Loyola* (Seuil, 1971).
90. Hocquenghem and Schérer, *L'Ame atomique*, p. 325.
91. Ibid., p. 324.
92. J.-F. Lyotard, 'Answering the Question: What is Postmodernism?', translated by R. Durand, in *The Postmodern Condition: a Report on Knowledge* (Manchester University Press, 1984) p. 76.
93. Ibid., pp. 81–2.
94. Hocquenghem and Schérer, *L'Ame atomique*, pp. 175–6.
95. Ibid., p. 128.
96. Ibid., p. 304.
97. Ibid., p. 30.
98. R. Schérer, 'Angelus novus', in *Pari sur l'impossible: études fouriéristes* (Presses universitaires de Vincennes, 1989) pp. 211–13. Also in: *Gai Pied Hebdo*, no. 334 (10 September, 1988).
99. Hocquenghem and Bory, *Comment nous appelez-vous déjà?*, p. 195. My emphasis.

Chapter 4: Fictions

1. G. Hocquenghem, *Fin de section* (Christian Bourgois, 1975) p. 17.
2. For more on *l'affaire Coral*, see *Le Monde*, 18 November 1982, p. 9; 19 November 1982, p. 12; 21–2 November, p. 7; 26 November 1982, p. 2; 22 January 1983, p. 12.
3. Hocquenghem and Schérer, *L'Ame atomique*, p. 28.
4. 'Oùen est l'homosexualité en 85, ou pourquoi je ne veux pas être un "écrivain gay"', *Masques*, nos 25–6 (Spring–Summer 1985) pp. 111–13.
5. Hocquenghem, *La Beauté du métis*, p. 75.
6. Ibid., p. 77. For an alternative, rhizomatic image, see that of the 'fairy rings' (*ronds de sorcière*) which pertain to the dispersal of 'homosexuality' towards its edges, 'linked between them by the inextricable network of mycelium': Hocquenghem, *La Dérive*, p. 20.
7. Deleuze and Guattari, *L'Anti-Oedipe*, p. 442.
8. G. Hocquenghem, *Love in Relief*, translated by M. Whisler (New York: SeaHorse Press, 1986) p. 34.
9. Hocquenghem and Schérer, *L'Ame atomique*, p. 109.
10. Hocquenghem, *Love in Relief*, p. 204.
11. Ibid., p. 29.
12. Ibid., p. 124.
13. Ibid., p. 166.
14. Ibid., p. 63.

15. D. Haraway, 'A Manifesto for Cyborgs: Science, Technology, and Socialist Feminism in the 1980s', in E. Weed (ed.) *Coming to Terms: Feminism, Theory, Politics* (Routledge, 1989) p. 187.

16. Hocquenghem, *Love in Relief*, p. 164.

17. Deleuze and Guattari, *Anti-Oedipus*, pp. 132–3.

18. Hocquenghem, *Love in Relief*, p. 238.

19. W. Woodhull, *Transfigurations of the Maghreb: Feminism, Decolonization, and Literatures* (University of Minnesota Press, 1993) p. 196.

20. Hocquenghem, *Love in Relief*, p. 201.

21. Ibid., p. 112.

22. Ibid., p. 12.

23. Ibid., p. 192.

24. Ibid., p. 147.

25. Ibid., pp. 114–15.

26. Hocquenghem considered that the *roman-feuilleton* was the only one appropriate to the *romanesque d'enfance* (novel of childhood): G. Hocquenghem, 'James-Stevenson', *Recherches*, no. 23 (June 1976) pp. 200–4.

27. F. Moretti, *The Way of the World: The Bildungsroman in European Culture* (Verso, 1987) pp. 166–7.

28. L. Edelman, 'The Mirror and the Tanks: "AIDS", Subjectivity, and the Rhetoric of Activism', in T. Murphy and S. Poirier (eds), *Writing AIDS: Gay Literature, Language and Analysis* (Columbia University Press, 1993) pp. 9–38.

29. See the interview with Schérer and Hennig, 'La Constellation Hocquenghem', *Gai Pied Hebdo*, no. 396 (30 November 1989) pp. 66–7.

30. Hocquenghem, *Love in Relief*, p. 205.

31. G. Hocquenghem, *Eve* (Albin Michel, 1987) p. 311.

32. Hocquenghem and Schérer, *Co-ire*, p. 101.

33. Ibid., p. 128.

34. Hocquenghem, *Eve*, p. 64.

35. Eve's connection with the Virgin Islands; the 'nativity' scene at the birth of the second Adam, ibid., p. 305.

36. Ibid., pp. 78, 305.

37. Ibid., pp. 145–7.

38. Ibid., pp. 119, 139.

39. Plato, *The Symposium*, translated by W. Hamilton (Harmondsworth: Penguin, 1951) p. 60.

40. Hocquenghem, *Eve*, p. 96.

41. See: R. Lapsley and M. Westlake, 'From *Casablanca* to *Pretty Woman*: the politics of romance', *Screen*, vol. 33, no. 1 (Spring 1992) pp. 27–49.

42. Hocquenghem, *Eve*, p. 167.

43. Ibid., p. 273.

44. Hocquenghem, *La Dérive*, p. 107.
45. See Chapter 1, note 19.
46. Hocquenghem, *Eve*, p. 169.
47. G. Hocquenghem, *Le Gay Voyage: guide homosexuel des grandes métropoles* (Albin Michel, 1980) includes a final section on ancient Alexandria ('Alexandrie imaginaire'). See also the early short story on the burning of the Library of Alexandria: 'Eloge du pompier', *La Revue*, no. 1 (April–May 1978) pp. 3–6.
48. H. Bhabha, 'DissemiNation: time, narrative, and the margins of the modern nation', in H. Bhabha (ed.), *Nation and Narration* (Routledge, 1990) pp. 291–322.
49. G. Hocquenghem, *La Colère de l'agneau* (Albin Michel, 1985) p. 548.
50. Ibid., p. 266.
51. Hocquenghem and Schérer, *L'Ame atomique*, p. 316.
52. Ibid., p. 318.
53. S. Kierkegaard, *Either/Or: a Fragment of Life*, translated by A. Hannay (Harmondsworth: Penguin, 1992) pp. 497–500.
54. Hocquenghem and Schérer, *L'Ame atomique*, p. 75.
55. G. Hocquenghem, *Les Voyages et aventures extraordinaires du frère Angelo* (Albin Michel, 1988) pp. 163–4.
56. Ibid., p. 165.
57. Ibid., p. 187.
58. Ibid., pp. 238–9.
59. T. Todorov, *La Conquête de l'Amérique: la question de l'autre* (Seuil, 1982).
60. Hocquenghem, *Les Voyages*, p. 166.
61. Ibid., pp. 250–1.
62. Ibid., p. 282.
63. Ibid., p. 213.
64. Ibid., p. 127.
65. See for example the obituary by Laurent Joffrin: 'Guy Hocquenghem, La Mort de l'ange', *Libération*, 30 August 1988, pp. 28–30.
66. Hocquenghem, *Les Voyages*, p. 309.

Chapter 5: Presence

1. G. Hocquenghem, *L'Amphithéâtre des morts: Mémoires anticipées* (Gallimard, 1994) p. 80.
2. Ibid., p. 38.
3. Ibid., p. 66.
4. Ibid., p. 59.
5. E. Sedgwick, *Epistemology of the Closet* (Berkeley, University of California Press, 1990) p. 1.

6. S. Watney, 'The French Connection', *Sight and Sound*, vol. 3, no. 6 (June 1993) pp. 24–5.
7. Hocquenghem, *L'Après-mai des faunes*, p. 197.
8. Hocquenghem, *La Dérive*, p. 85.
9. G. Hocquenghem, 'L'homosexualité est-elle un vice guérissable?', *Gai Pied Hebdo*, nos 278–9 (11 August 1987) pp. 64–5.
10. E. Sedgwick, *Tendencies* (Routledge, 1994) p. 8.
11. J. Butler, *Bodies that Matter: On the discursive limits of 'sex'* (Routledge, 1993) p. 230.
12. Anonymous, 'Les Culs énergumènes', *Recherches*, (March 1973) pp. 226–65.
13. Hocquenghem and Schérer, *L'Ame atomique*, p. 255.
14. Ibid., p. 253.
15. Ibid., p. 258.
16. Ibid., p. 261.
17. Ibid., p. 217.
18. T. De Lauretis, *Technologies of Gender: Essays on Theory: Film and Fiction* (Macmillan, 1989), p. 15.
19. A. Bjørnerud, 'Outing Barthes: Barthes and the Quest(ion) of (a Gay) Identity Politics', *New Formations*, no. 18 (Winter 1992) pp. 122–41.
20. D. Morton, 'Birth of the Cyberqueer', *PMLA*, vol. 110, no. 3 (May 1995) pp. 369–81.

Bibliography

Works by Guy Hocquenghem

This does not pretend to be an exhaustive list, but includes all published volumes, important articles not in volumes, as well as articles invoked in the text.

Le Désir homosexuel (Jean-Pierre Delarge, 1972). *Homosexual Desire*, translated by D. Dangoor, with a new introduction by Michael Moon, preface by Jeffrey Weeks (Duke University Press, 1993).

L'Après-mai des faunes: Volutions, preface by G. Deleuze (Grasset, 1974).

Fin de section (Christian Bourgois, 1975).

With R. Schérer: *Co-ire: album systématique de l'enfance*, *Recherches*, no. 22 (1976).

'James-Stevenson', *Recherches*, no. 23 (June 1976) pp. 200–4.

La Dérive homosexuelle (Jean-Pierre Delarge, 1977). 'Aux pédérastes incompréhensibles' appears as 'Towards an Irrecuperable Pederasty', translated by C. Fox, in J. Goldberg (ed.), *Reclaiming Sodom* (Routledge, 1994) pp. 233–46.

With J.-L. Bory: *Comment nous appelez-vous déjà? Ces hommes que l'on dit homosexuels* (Calmann-Lévy, 1977).

'Subversion et décadence du mâle d'après-Mai', *Autrement*, no. 12 (1978) pp. 157–64.

'Eloge du pompier', *La Revue*, no. 1 (April–May 1978) pp. 3–6.

La Beauté du métis: réflexions d'un francophobe (Ramsay, 1979).

With M. Foucault and J. Danet: 'Fous d'enfance: qui a peur des pédophiles?', *Recherches*, nos 36–7 (April 1979) pp. 69–82.

Race d'Ep! Un siècle d'images de l'homosexualité (Libres-Hallier, 1979). The film is co-written with, and directed by, Lionel Soukaz.

Le Gay Voyage: guide homosexuel des grandes métropoles (Albin Michel, 1980).

Preface to H. de Balzac, *Monographie de la presse parisienne* (Hallier/Albin Michel, 1981).

Preface to H. Heger, *Les Hommes au triangle rose* (Persona, 1981).

L'Amour en relief (Albin Michel, 1982). *Love in Relief,* translated by M. Whisler, preface by G. Stambolian (SeaHorse Press, 1986).
With J.-L. Hennig: *Les Français de la honte: la morale des Français racontée par eux-mêmes* (Albin Michel, 1983).
Les Petits Garçons (Albin Michel, 1983).
La Colère de l'agneau (Albin Michel, 1985).
'Où en est l'homosexualité en 85, ou pourquoi je ne veux pas être un "écrivain gay"', *Masques,* nos 25–6 (Spring–Summer 1985) pp. 111–13.
With R. Schérer: *L'Ame atomique: pour une esthétique d'ère nucléaire* (Albin Michel, 1986).
Lettre ouverte à ceux qui sont passes dua col Mao au Rotary (Albin Michel, 1986).
L'Europe des villes rêvées: Vienne (Autrement, 1986).
Eve (Albin Michel, 1987).
'L'homosexualité est-elle un vice guérissable?', *Gai Pied Hebdo,* nos 278–9 (11 August 1987) pp. 64–5.
'Le Captif délivré', *Gai Pied Hebdo,* no. 334 (10 September 1988) p. 55.
'La volonté d'écart', *Sociétés,* no. 21 (December 1988) pp. 3–4.
Les Voyages et aventures extraordinaires du frère Angelo (Albin Michel, 1988).
L'Amphithéâtre des morts: mémoires anticipées, preface by R. Surzur, afterword by R. Schérer (Gallimard, 1994).

Secondary sources

'La Constellation Hocquenghem', *Gai Pied Hebdo,* no. 396 (30 November 1989) pp. 66–7.
Présence de Guy Hocquenghem (*Cahiers de l'imaginaire*/L'Harmattan, 1992).
'Trois Milliards de pervers: Grande Encyclopédie des homosexualités', preface by F. Guattari, *Recherches* (March 1973).

Allorent I. 'Etude de quelques mythes dans *Eve* d'Hocquenghem', *Recherches sur l'imaginaire,* no. 22 (1991) pp. 13–31.
Althusser, L. and Balibar, E. *Reading Capital,* translated by Ben Brewster (NLB, 1970).
Althusser, L. *Lenin and Philosophy and Other Essays,* translated by Ben Brewster (NLB, 1971).
Bach, G. 'Celui qui ne s'est pas renié', *Cahiers du féminisme,* no. 46 (Autumn 1988) pp. 36–7.
Bakhtin, M. *Rabelais and His World,* translated by H. Iswolsky (MIT Press, 1968).
Barthes, R. *Sade, Fourier, Loyola* (Seuil, 1971).

Baudrillard, J. *A l'ombre des majorités silencieuses* (Denoël/Gonthier, 1982). *In the Shadow of the Silent Majorities*, translated by P. Patton, et al. (Semiotext(e), 1983).

Beecher, J. and Bienvenu, R. (eds) *The Utopian Vision of Charles Fourier: on Work, Love and Passionate Attraction* (Jonathan Cape, 1972).

Benjamin, W. *Illuminations*, translated by H. Zohn (Fontana/Collins, 1973).

Berman, M. *All That Is Solid Melts Into Air: The Experience of Modernity* (Verso, 1983).

Bhabha, H. 'DissemiNation: time, narrative, and the margins of the modern nation', in H. Bhabha (ed.) *Nation and Narration* (Routledge, 1990) pp. 291–322.

Bjørnerud, A. 'Outing Barthes: Barthes and the Quest(ion) of (a Gay) Identity Politics', *New Formations*, no. 18 (Winter 1992) pp. 122–41.

Boulé, J.-P. (ed.) *Hervé Guibert, Nottingham French Studies*, vol. 34, no. 1 (Spring 1995).

Boundas, C.V. and Olkowski, D. (eds) *Gilles Deleuze and the Theater of Philosophy* (Routledge, 1994).

Braidotti, R. *Patterns of Dissonance: a Study of Women in Contemporary Philosophy*, translated by E. Guild (Polity Press, 1991).

Butler, J. *Subjects of Desire: Hegelian Reflections in Twentieth-Century France* (Columbia University Press, 1987).

—— *Bodies that Matter: On the discursive limits of 'sex'* (Routledge, 1993).

Cruikshank, M. *The Gay and Lesbian Liberation Movement* (Routledge, 1992).

Debray, R. *Modeste contribution aux discours et cérémonies du dixième anniversaire* (Maspero, 1978). 'A Modest Contribution to the Rules and Ceremonies of the Tenth Anniversary', *New Left Review*, no. 115 (May–June 1979) pp. 45–65.

De Ceccatty, R. 'L'écrivain Guy Hocquenghem est mort: "La Beauté du métis"', *Le Monde*, 30 August 1988, p. 34.

De Certeau, M. 'Walking in the City', in S. During (ed.) *The Cultural Studies Reader* (Routledge, 1993).

D'Eaubonne, F. 'Bonne nuit, cher prince', *Gai Pied Hebdo*, no. 334 (10 September 1988) p. 54.

De Lauretis, T. *Technologies of Gender: Essays on Theory, Film and Fiction* (Macmillan, 1989).

Deleuze, G. *Différence et répétition* (Presses universitaires de France, 1968), *Difference and Repetition*, translated by P. Patton (Athlone, 1994).

—— 'Pensée nomade', in Centre culturel international de Cerisy-la-salle, *Nietzsche aujourd'hui. I. Intensités* (Union générale des écrivains, 1973).

Deleuze, G. and Guattari, F. *L'Anti-Oedipe: capitalisme et schizo-phrénie* (Minuit, 1972). *Anti-Oedipus: Capitalism and Schizophrenia* translated by R. Hurley, M. Seem, and H. Lane (Athlone Press, 1984).

D'Emilio, J. *Sexual Politics, Sexual Communities: The Making of a Homosexual Minority in the United States 1940–1970* (University of Chicago Press, 1983).

Dews, P. *Logics of Disintegration: Post-Structuralist Thought and the Claims of Critical Theory* (Verso, 1987).

Diderot, D. *Lettre sur les aveugles* (Garnier-Flammarion, 1972).

—— *Le Neveu de Rameau et autres dialogues philosophiques* (Gallimard, 1972). *Rameau's Nephew*, translated by L. Tancock (Penguin, 1976).

Dollimore, J. *Sexual Dissidence: Augustine to Wilde, Freud to Foucault* (Oxford University Press, 1991).

Duberman, M. *Stonewall* (Dutton, 1993).

Eagleton, T. *Walter Benjamin or Towards a Revolutionary Criticism* (Verso, 1981).

—— *The Ideology of the Aesthetic* (Blackwell, 1990).

FHAR. *Rapport contre la normalité* (Champ libre, 1971).

Fletcher, J. 'Psychoanalysis and Gay Theory', in S. Shepherd and M. Wallis (eds) *Coming on Strong: Gay Politics and Culture* (Unwin Hyman, 1989) pp. 90–118.

Foucault, M. *Histoire de la folie à l'âge classique* (Plon, 1961). *Madness and Civilisation*, translated by R. Howard (Tavistock, 1967).

—— *Surveiller et punir* (Gallimard, 1975). *Discipline and Punish*, translated by A. Sheridan (Allen Lane, 1977).

—— *Histoire de la sexualité. I. La Volonté de savoir* (Gallimard, 1976). *History of Sexuality. Vol. 1: An Introduction*, translated by R. Hurley (Allen Lane, 1979).

Freud, S. 'Three Essays on Sexuality', in *Standard Edition of the Complete Psychological Works*, translated by J. Strachey and A. Freud, vol. 7 (Hogarth Press, 1953).

—— 'Psychoanalytic Notes on an Autobiographical Account of a Case of Paranoia', *Standard Edition*, vol. 12 (Hogarth Press, 1958).

—— 'Femininity', *Standard Edition*, vol. 22 (Hogarth Press, 1964).

Fuss, D. *Essentially Speaking: Feminism, Nature and Difference* (Routledge, 1990).

Giddens, A. *The Consequences of Modernity* (Polity Press, 1990).

—— *The Transformation of Intimacy: Sexuality, Love and Eroticism in Modern Societies* (Polity Press, 1992).

Girard, J. *Le Mouvement homosexuel en France 1945–1980* (Syros, 1981).

Guibert, H. *Des Aveugles* (Gallimard, 1985).

—— *A l'ami qui ne m'a pas sauvé la vie* (Gallimard, 1990). *To The Friend Who Did Not Save My Life*, translated by L. Coverdale (Quartet, 1991).

—— *Le Protocole compassionnel* (Gallimard, 1991). *The Compassion Protocol*, translated by J. Kirkup (Quartet, 1993).

Hamon, H. and Rotman, P. *Génération: les années de rêve* (Seuil, 1987).

Hanley, D. and Kerr, A.P. (eds) *May '68: Coming of Age* (Macmillan, 1989).

Hanley, D., Kerr, A.P. and Waites, N., *Contemporary France: Politics and Society since 1945* (Routledge, 1984).

Haraway, D. 'A Manifesto for Cyborgs: Science, Technology, and Socialist Feminism in the 1980s', in E. Weed (ed.) *Coming to Terms: Feminism, Theory, Politics* (Routledge, 1989).

Heath, S. *Questions of Cinema* (Macmillan, 1981).

Hennig, J.-L. 'Le gay voyageur', *Gai Pied Hebdo*, no. 334 (10 September 1988) p. 53.

Hewitt, N. (ed.) *The Culture of Reconstruction: European Literature, Thought and Film 1945–50* (Macmillan, 1989).

Jardine, A. *Gynesis: Configurations of Woman and Modernity* (Cornell University Press, 1985).

Joffrin, L. *Un Coup de jeune: portrait d'une génération morale* (Arlea, 1987).

—— 'Guy Hocquenghem, La Mort de l'ange', *Libération*, 30 August 1988, pp. 28–30.

Kant, I. 'Perpetual Peace: a Philosophical Sketch', in *Political Writings*, translated by H.B. Nisbet (Cambridge University Press, 1991).

Kierkegaard, S. *Either/Or: a Fragment of Life*, translated by A. Hannay (Penguin, 1992).

Kristeva, J. *Etranger à nous-mêmes* (Fayard, 1988). *Strangers to Ourselves*, translated by L. Rondiel (Harvester Wheatsheaf, 1991).

Landel, V. 'Hocquenghem contre le dogme', *Magazine littéraire*, no. 258 (October 1988) pp. 92–3.

Lapsley, R. and Westlake, M. 'From *Casablanca* to *Pretty Woman*: the politics of romance', *Screen*, vol. 33, no. 1 (Spring 1992) pp. 27–49.

Leclair, O. 'Oiseau de la nuit', *Sociétés*, no. 21 (December 1988) pp. 43–5.

Lejeune, P. *Le Pacte autobiographique* (Seuil, 1975).

Lévy, J. and Nouss, A. *Sida-Fiction: essai d'anthologie romanesque* (Presses universitaires de Lyon, 1994).

Lipovetsky, G. *L'Ere du vide: essais sur l'individualisme contemporain* (Gallimard, 1983)

Lucretius. *On the Nature of the Universe*, translated by R.E. Latham (Penguin, 1994).

Lyotard, J.-F. *La Condition postmoderne* (Minuit, 1979). *The Postmodern Condition: a Report on Knowledge*, translated by G. Bennington and B. Massumi (Manchester University Press, 1984).

—— 'Réponse à la question: qu'est-ce que le postmoderne?', *Critique* (April 1982) pp. 357–67. 'Answering the Question: What is Postmodernism?', in ibid., pp. 71–82.

Marcuse, H. *One-Dimensional Man* (Ark, 1986).

Marsan, H. 'Un Homme du présent', *Gai Pied Hebdo*, no. 334 (10 September 1988) pp. 53–4.

Massumi, B. *A User's Guide to Capitalism and Schizophrenia: Deviations from Deleuze and Guattari* (MIT Press, 1992).

Mieli, M. *Homosexuality and Liberation: Elements of a Gay Critique*, translated by D. Fernbach (Gay Men's Press, 1980).

Moretti, F. *The Way of the World: The Bildungsroman in European Culture* (Verso, 1987).

Morton, D. 'Birth of the Cyberqueer', *PMLA*, vol. 110, no. 3 (May 1995) pp. 369–81.

Murphy, T. and Poirier, S (eds) *Writing AIDS: Gay Literature, Language and Analysis* (Columbia University Press, 1993).

Ory, P. *L'Entre-deux-mai. Histoire culturelle de la France Mai 1968–Mai 1981* (Seuil, 1983).

—— *L'Aventure culturelle française* (Flammarion, 1989).

Plant, S. *The Most Radical Gesture: The Situationist International in a Postmodern Age* (Routledge, 1992)

Plato. *The Symposium*, translated by W. Hamilton (Penguin, 1951)

Povert, L. 'Le dernier fils d'Ep?', *Gai Pied Hebdo*, no. 333 (3 September 1988) pp. 8–10.

Reader, K. *Intellectuals and the Left in France since 1968* (Macmillan, 1987).

—— *The May 1968 Events in France: Reproductions and Interpretations* (Macmillan, 1993).

Reich, W. *The Mass Psychology of Fascism*, translated by V. Carfagno (Penguin, 1975).

Robinson, C. *Scandal in the Ink: Male and Female Homosexuality in Twentieth-Century French Literature* (Cassell, 1995).

Salvaresi, E. *Mai en héritage: 14 portraits, 490 itinéraires* (Syros/Alternatives, 1988).

Schérer, R. (ed.), *Charles Fourier ou la contestation globale*, (Seghers, 1970).

—— *Pari sur l'impossible: études fouriéristes* (Presses universitaires de Vincennes, 1989).

—— 'Guy Hocquenghem: la passion de l'étranger', *Sociétés*, no. 21 (December 1988) pp. 46–50.

Sedgwick, E. *Epistemology of the Closet* (University of California Press, 1990).

—— *Tendencies* (Routledge, 1994).

Simpson, M. 'Backs to the Wall', *Time Out*, 9–16 March 1994, p. 91.

Stambolian, G. and Marks, E. (eds) *Homosexualities and French Literature: Cultural Contexts, Critical Texts* (Cornell University Press, 1979).

Todorov, T. *La Conquête de l'Amérique: la question de l'autre* (Seuil, 1982). *The Conquest of America: the Question of the Other*, translated by R. Howard (Harper Perennial, 1992).

Touraine, A. *Le Mouvement de mai ou le communisme utopique* (Seuil, 1968).

—— *Mouvements sociaux d'aujourd'hui: acteurs et analystes* (Ouvrières, 1982).

Tournier, M. *Les Météores* (Gallimard, 1975). *Gemini*, translated by A. Carter (Collins, 1981).

Trilling, L. *Sincerity and Authenticity* (Oxford University Press, 1972).

Turkle, S. *Psychoanalytic Politics: Freud's French Revolution* (Burnett Books, 1979).

Walker, B. *Gnosticism: Its History and Influence* (Crucible Press, 1989).

Watney, S. 'The French Connection', *Sight and Sound*, vol. 3, no. 6 (June 1993) pp. 24–5.

Weeks, J. *Sexuality and Its Discontents* (Routledge, 1985).

Woodhull, W. *Transfigurations of the Maghreb: Feminism, Decolonization and Literatures* (University of Minnesota Press, 1993).

Index